D0574863

THE
desserts
COOKBOOK

SOUTHERN LIVING
PROGRESSIVE FARMER

Favorite Recipes Press © MCMLXXI
Library of Congress Catalog
Card Number 78-162980

contents

preface

Southern homemakers know that desserts may be made in imaginative shapes and delectable flavors. There are delicious cakes with surprise fillings and melt-in-your mouth frostings . . . creamy smooth puddings . . . nutritious fresh fruit . . . the variety is endless. Desserts, in their infinite variety, offer the creative homemaker innumerable opportunities to finish her meals with a flourish.

When the main course features a roast with all the trimmings, end with a light touch — custard or a fruit-filled tart. If a casserole is the basis of your supper, add excitement with a lemon ice box dessert or the family's favorite sweet bread. On hot summer evenings, combine icy cold citrus fruits in the classic southern dessert, ambrosia. And for those extra-special occasions, offer elegant desserts — Baked Alaska or a Creme Brulee.

Now the wonderfully varied world of dessert cookery is captured for you in *Southern Living's* DESSERTS COOKBOOK. Featuring favorite dessert recipes from hundreds of southern homemakers, this cookbook brings together in one volume the very best home-tested, family-approved dishes. Cakes . . . cookies . . . pies . . . puddings . . . frozen desserts . . . fruit desserts . . . sweet breads . . . all are included.

From the kitchens of *Southern Living's* readers to you and your family comes an invitation to have a delightful dessert — southern style.

ABBREVIATIONS USED IN THIS BOOK

Teaspoon . . . . . .tsp.		Large . . . . . . .lge.	
Tablespoon . . . . tbsp.		Package . . . . . pkg.	
Cup . . . . c.		Small . . . . . .sm.	
Ounce . . . . oz.		Pint . . . . pt.	
Pound . . . . lb.		Quart . . . . qt.	
Dozen . . . . . . doz.		Gallon . . . . . . .gal.	

EQUIVALENTS

3 tsp. = 1 tbsp.

2 tbsp. = 1/8 c.

4 tbsp. = 1/4 c.

8 tbsp. = 1/2 c.

16 tbsp. = 1 c.

5 tbsp. + 1 tsp. = 1/3 c.

12 tbsp. = 3/4 c.

4 oz. = 1/2 c.

8 oz. = 1 c.

4 3/4 to 5 c. sifted cake flour = 1 lb.

2 c. = 1 pt.

2 c. sugar = 1 lb.

5/8 c. = 1/2 c. + 2 tbsp.

7/8 c. = 3/4 c. + 2 tbsp.

1 lb. butter = 2 c. or 4 sticks

2 pt. = 1 qt.

1 qt. = 4 c.

A few grains (also a speck) = Less than 1/8 tsp.

Pinch = As much as can be taken between tip of finger and thumb

1 oz. = 2 tbsp. fat or liquid

2 c. fat = 1 lb.

4 c. sifted all-purpose flour = 1 lb.

SUBSTITUTIONS

1 tablespoon cornstarch (for thickening) = 2 tablespoons flour (approximately)

1 c. sifted all-purpose flour = 1 cup plus 2 tablespoons sifted cake flour

1 square chocolate (ounce) = 3 or 4 tablespoons cocoa plus 1/2 tablespoon fat

1 teaspoon baking powder = 1/4 teaspoon baking soda plus 1/2 teaspoon cream

1 teaspoon baking powder = 1/4 teaspoon baking soda plus 1/2 teaspoon cream of tartar

1 cup bottled milk = 1/2 cup evaporated milk plus 1/2 c. water

1 c. sour milk = 1 cup sweet milk into which 1 tablespoon vinegar or lemon juice has been stirred; or 1 cup buttermilk

1 c. sweet milk = 1 cup sour milk or buttermilk plus 1/2 teaspoon baking soda

1 cup cream, sour, heavy = 1/3 cup butter and 2/3 cup milk in any sour-milk recipe

1 c. cream, sour, thin = 3 tablespoons butter and 3/4 cup milk in sour-milk recipe

1 c. molasses = 1 cup honey

HERBS AND SPICES FOR DESSERTS

Herbs and spices can play an important role in dessert-making. They can be used to complement the main ingredients and greatly enhance the overall appeal of your dessert. Here are a few of the common herbs and spices you will enjoy using in a variety of desserts.

Allspice is a pungent and sharply aromatic spice. It combines the flavors of cinnamon, cloves, nutmeg, and juniper berries. Allspice is available in both whole and ground form. It is preferable to buy it whole and grind it just before using. It is usually used in combination with other spices in fruit desserts, cakes, and pies.

Anise, a sweet-smelling herb, has a delicious subtle licorice flavor. Anise seeds are frequently used in cookies and fruit desserts. To release their full flavor, crush them with a rolling pin just before using. Commercially-extracted anise oil is used to flavor cakes, coffee cakes, and sweet-breads.

Caraway, a delightfully-flavored and spicy-smelling herb that is a classic addition to coffee cakes and cookies. Like anise seeds, caraway seeds should be crushed to release their full flavor.

Cardamon is a spice that can be used as you do cinnamon and cloves. It is excellent either alone or in combination with other spices. It is particularly good in recipes calling for honey. Cardamon loses flavor very quickly. Therefore it should be freshly ground each time it is used.

Cinnamon is one of the most popular dessert spices in American kitchens. It is also one of the oldest spices known to man. In stick form or powdered, its sweet aromatic flavor is excellent in fruit compotes, cookies, cakes, pies, and rice pudding.

Clove, another popular spice, is available in whole or powdered form. Clove is most often used sparingly in combination with other spices. Too much clove will produce an unattractive color and bitter taste. It is particularly nice in fruit desserts, pies, cakes, cookies, and some puddings.

Coriander seed is an herb. These seeds are a delightful addition to pastries and sweets and are used in much the same way as caraway seeds.

Fennel, another herb, has a hot, sweet flavor. Fennel comes in seed form and adds zest to pies and baked fruit desserts.

Ginger, a classic spice, is available in many forms: root, syrup, candied, and ground. The latter form is commonly used in cookies, cakes, fruits, pies, and puddings. It is delightful alone or in combination with other spices.

Mace is a spice closely related to nutmeg. It is usually ground and is especially good in pastry. Its nutlike flavor is an excellent complement to cherry and chocolate desserts.

Mint is one of our best-loved herbs. The range of mint flavors includes peppermint, spearmint, apple, orange, and pineapple mints. Mint leaves should be crushed just before using. Uncrushed leaves are an excellent garnish. The oil, extracted from crushed leaves, should be used very sparingly — a drop at a time. Mint is a marvelous addition to fruit cups, ices, chocolate desserts, and apple combinations.

Nutmeg is an all-time favorite spice. It adds a delightful flavor to pastry and dessert dough mixtures. The flavor of nutmeg is best when it is freshly ground in a special nutmeg mill, similar to a pepper mill.

Poppy seed is a spice frequently used in coffee cakes, pie crusts, and cookies. The seeds are best when roasted or steamed, then crushed. If you use them often, it may be worth investing in a mill to grind the seeds.

Saffron is a flavorful herb with a rich yellow color. It adds its own distinctive taste to sweet breads and cakes. It also makes a nice coloring for candies. Use sparingly: it is the most expensive of all herbs and spices.

Sesame seed, with nut-like flavor, makes a good topping for sweet breads, cookies, and coffee cakes. This herb tastes best when lightly toasted for about 20 minutes in a 350-degree oven. Stir the seeds frequently while toasting.

COOKING TERMS AND DEFINITIONS

a la Mode . . . . Served with a topping of ice cream

au Lait . . . . A beverage made and served with milk

Bake . . . . To cook by dry heat in an oven

Bavarian . . . . Pudding made with a gelatin-cream base

Beat . . . . To whip with a spoon, hand beater, or electric mixer in order to combine food or incorporate air

Blancmange . . . . A milk dessert, flavored and thickened with cornstarch, flour, or gelatin and usually shaped in a mold

Blend . . . . To mix ingredients until thoroughly combined

Bombe . . . . A frozen dessert of two or more mixtures (such as ice cream or sherbet) packed into a melon-shaped mold

Bonbon . . . . A sweet made of or dipped into fondant

Candy . . . . To cook fruit and fruit peel in heavy syrup until transparent and plump

Caramel . . . . Burnt sugar syrup used for flavor and color

Caramelize . . . . To heat dry sugar until melted, lightly browned, and caramel-flavored

Charlotte . . . . Usually a gelatin dessert with flavored whipped cream, molded in a form lined with strips of cake or ladyfingers

Coat-the-Spoon . . . . . . To cook until a mixture adheres in a thin layer to a metal stirring spoon

Cobbler . . . . A deep dish fruit pie made with a rich pastry or biscuit dough top

Cream . . . . To work or beat shortening until light and fluffy. Sugar and/or flour and eggs may be creamed into the shortening

Custard . . . . A cooked or baked mixture consisting mainly of eggs, milk, and sugar

Cut . . . . To combine shortening with flour and other dry ingredients by chopping it into the mixture with two knives or spatulas

Dissolve . . . . To melt or liquefy

Dredge . . . . To coat with flour or other finely ground coating

Eclair	A small custard or whipped cream-filled, finger-shaped pastry
Fold	To combine ingredients by blending with a spoon or wire whisk, using an up-and-over motion
Glaze	To coat with a thin sugar syrup or to cover with a thin icing
Ice	A sweet frozen dessert of fruit juice, water, and sugar
Kisses	Tiny dessert meringues
Knead	To manipulate dough or pastry with the hands in a pressing motion that incorporates folding and stretching
Macaroons	Small cakes made from egg whites, sugar, and ground almonds or almond paste
Meringue	Stiffly beaten egg white-sugar mixture used as a pie topping or baked and served as a dessert shell
Mocha	Coffee or coffee-chocolate flavor
Parfait	Ice cream, fruit, and whipped cream layered dessert; or a frozen mixture of egg whites or yolks, cooked with hot syrup, and combined with whipped cream
Petits Fours	Small fancy tea cakes, usually frosted
Scald	To heat liquid to a temperature just below the boiling point. A thin skin forming over milk indicates that the scalding point has been reached
Sherbet	A fruit juice, sugar, egg white, and milk or water mixture which is frozen
Sift	To shake dry ingredients through a sieve or sifter
Simmer	To cook in liquid that is just below the boiling point
Torte	A cake or pastry made of many eggs, sugar, and often grated nuts or dry bread crumbs instead of flour and baked in several layer cake pans. Sometimes filled with jam and usually covered with frosting
Whip	To incorporate air into a mixture by beating rapidly by hand or with an electric mixer

cakes, frostings, & fillings

On special occasions of every kind, the center of attraction is certain to be a cake. Cakes just seem to belong in the middle of every fun-filled occasion from the Christmas holiday season to a summer wedding. In fact, cakes make the most ordinary gatherings seem extra-special. Try one the next time you want to perk up a meal — you'll agree!

Homemakers have long known that the secret to good cake making lies in having a tried and proven recipe . . . one that incorporates just the right balance of ingredients with that touch of creative cooking that makes the difference between ordinary food and great dishes. In this section, you will find dozens of such recipes from the kitchens of southern cooks. From imaginatively decorated birthday cakes to holiday fruitcakes bursting with plump fruit and flavorful nuts, they are all here. Recipes for light, melt-in-your-mouth angel food cakes, perfect for summertime eating . . . for richly-delicious chocolate cakes . . . for that all-time southern favorite, poundcake.

As you browse through these pages, imagine mixing and matching the endless variety of cakes with fillings and frostings. You're certain to enjoy creating your very own cake — and your family is certain to enjoy the results. Star a beautiful cake as the center of attraction at your next meal!

What gives a homemaker more pleasure than the sight and smell of a home-baked cake! And what gives her happy family more eating pleasure!

Cakes are of two basic types: those made with shortening – the butter, pound, fruit, and chiffon cakes – and those made without shortening – the angel and sponge cakes. The first group are usually baked in round, square, or sheet pans; the second are almost always baked in tube pans.

There are two methods used to make cakes with shortening. One is the *creaming method.* In this method, the shortening, sugar, eggs, and salt are creamed or blended together until they are light in color and smooth in texture. Then the dry ingredients and the liquid are added alternately and the entire mixture is blended until smooth. In the so-called *"quick" method,*

cooking methods

FOR CAKES, FROSTINGS, AND FILLINGS

shortening, the dry ingredients, and part of the liquid are mixed for two minutes, then the eggs and remaining liquid are added and the mixture is beaten for two minutes more.

The non-shortening cakes are usually prepared by beating the eggs thoroughly and adding the remaining ingredients in three or four parts.

CAKE INGREDIENTS

Flour: Your recipe tells you what kind of flour to use. In cake recipes the flour is always measured after sifting unless otherwise specified. If you substitute regular flour for cake flour, be sure to check the substitution rules on page 6. And never use self-rising flour as a substitute for either regular or cake flour.

Baking Powder: Most baking powders on the market today are double-action: the rising begins in the batter and continues during the baking process. For each cup of flour, use 1/2 teaspoon double-acting baking powder.

Shortening: Your recipe will specify the type of shortening to use – liquid, solid vegetable, or butter. If you substitute butter for other shortenings, reduce the amount of salt you use – butter is presalted.

Eggs: Eggs are important to produce a cake with fluffy texture. Always use medium eggs unless your recipe specifies otherwise. If you must substitute egg sizes, use two large eggs in place of every three medium ones.

CAKE PANS

After you have read the recipe and assembled your ingredients, turn your attention to the pans you will use. Unless otherwise specified, cake pans should be thoroughly greased and floured. (Here's a hint if you're making a chocolate cake. Instead of flour, use unsweetened cocoa — no white edges on your lovely dark cake!)

The pans you use may be metal or glass. Medium-weight metal pans which have shiny upper surfaces and dulled lower ones produce a thin, evenly browned cake crust. Glass or enamel cake pans will give a heavier, darker crust. And if you choose a glass pan, be sure to reduce your oven temperature by 25 degrees.

If you are making a cake which does not use shortening, you'll want a tube pan. These pans are not greased because the cake rises by clinging to the sides of the pan.

THE BAKING PROCESS

After you have prepared your cake batter, there are a few hints to follow for that just-right cake. First, whatever type of cake you are preparing, be sure to preheat the oven before you put in the cake to bake.

Fill cake pans one-half to two-thirds full. Before you bake shortening-type cakes, rap the pans sharply on the bottom with the palm of your hand. This will release air bubbles which could cause air pockets that would later make the cake split. If you are baking a non-shortening type cake, remove excess air by cutting through the batter with a spatula.

When you place cake pans in the oven, no pan should be directly over the other nor should pans touch each other or the wall of the oven.

When the cake is done, let it cool. Shortening-type cakes cool on cake racks in the pan for about 10 to 15 minutes, then are loosened and inverted on racks and let cool thoroughly. Non-shortening cakes should be inverted, preferably with the tube placed over a funnel, and let hang until cold.

FINISHING THE CAKE

To finish your cake, you'll want to frost or ice it and perhaps even fill it. Many homemakers are confused about the difference between frosting and icing. An icing is a glaze and is usually uncooked — it looks like a covering of ice, thus the name. Frostings are thicker and more opaque.

If you fill your cake, spread the filling between the layers before you frost them.

When applying frosting, be sure to have cake free of loose crumbs. And be certain that the frosting is cool enough not to soak into the cake!

For the actual frosting process, it is best to use a turntable. If you don't have one, set the cake plate on a large bowl with the plate extending beyond the bowl's rim. Turn the bowl while frosting the cake.

In the pages that follow, you'll find recipes for delicious cakes and the fabulous frostings and fillings which are so important in making your cake a feast for the eyes — as well as the appetite!

TIPSY CHERRY PARSON

2 pkg. dessert topping mix
1 c. cold milk
1 c. powdered sugar
1   8-oz. package cream cheese

1 baked angel food cake
Slivered toasted almonds
Slivered maraschino cherries

Combine the dessert topping and milk in a bowl and beat well. Add the powdered sugar gradually. Soften the cream cheese and beat into topping mixture, small amount at a time. Cut the cake into 3 layers. Place 1 layer on a cake plate and spread with layer of topping mixture. Repeat with remaining cake and part of the topping mixture. Frost top and sides with remaining topping mixture and decorate sides with almonds and cherries. Refrigerate until chilled. Garnish with stemmed cherries.

COFFEE ANGEL FOOD CAKE

1 1/2 c. sifted sugar
1 c. sifted cake flour
1/2 tsp. salt
1 1/4 c. egg whites

1 1/2 tsp. cream of tartar
1/2 tsp. vanilla
1 tbsp. instant coffee

Combine 1/2 cup sugar and flour and sift 4 times. Add salt to egg whites in a mixing bowl and beat until foamy. Sprinkle with cream of tartar and beat until soft peaks form. Add remaining sugar, 1/4 cup at a time, and beat until stiff peaks form. Fold in the vanilla and coffee. Fold in flour mixture, 1/2 cup at a time. Pour into ungreased 10-inch tube pan. Bake at 350 degrees for 35 to 45 minutes. Remove from oven and invert the pan on a rack.

Butter Icing

1/2 c. butter	1 tsp. vanilla
1/4 tsp. salt	2 tbsp. instant coffee
2 1/2 c. confectioners' sugar	Slivered toasted almonds
3 to 4 tbsp. milk	

Cream the butter and salt in a bowl. Sift the sugar and add to the creamed mixture, small amount at a time, beating well after each addition. Add enough milk for spreading consistency and mix well. Add the vanilla and coffee and beat until light and fluffy. Spread over cake and sprinkle generously with almonds.

Jeanette Peel Morrow, Graceville, Florida

COFFEE-CHOCOLATE CAKE

1 pkg. yellow cake mix	1 tsp. vanilla
1/4 c. brewed coffee	

Prepare cake mix according to package directions, using coffee as part of liquid, and add vanilla. Bake according to package directions.

Icing

3 tbsp. butter or margarine	Brewed coffee
1 sq. unsweetened chocolate	1 tsp. vanilla
1/2 box powdered sugar	

Brown the butter in a saucepan. Add the chocolate and stir until melted. Pour over powdered sugar in a bowl and mix, adding enough coffee until of spreading consistency. Add vanilla and spread on cake.

Mrs. Donald N. Jones, Tuila, Texas

CHERRY CAKE

1 can cherry pie filling	1 stick butter
1 pkg. white cake mix	

Place the pie filling in 8-inch square baking dish and pour cake mix over pie filling. Cut butter in thin slices and place over cake mix. Bake at 375 degrees for 35 to 40 minutes.

Mrs. Aruin Bone, Hopkinsville, Kentucky

LEMON-POPPY SEED CHIFFON CAKE

1/2 c. poppy seed	1 4-oz. package lemon pie
1/4 c. water	filling mix
1 pkg. lemon chiffon cake mix	1/2 c. heavy cream
1 tsp. grated lemon peel	

Soften the poppy seed in water for 1 to 2 hours. Prepare the cake mix according to package directions and stir in poppy seed. Pour into 2 ungreased 9-inch loaf pans. Bake according to package directions and cool. Prepare the pie filling mix according to package directions, reducing water by 1/2 cup and adding lemon peel. Cool. Cut 1 loaf horizontally into thirds. Other loaf may be used in favorite recipe or frozen. Whip the cream and fold into lemon filling. Spread on each layer and place layers together. Spread filling on top and sides of cake and chill before serving.

DELICIOUS APPLE CAKE

2 c. sugar	1 tsp. soda
2 eggs	3 c. peeled diced apples
1 1/2 c. salad oil	1 c. chopped pecans
3 c. flour	3/4 c. chopped red candied cherries
1 tsp. cinnamon	3/4 c. shredded coconut
1/2 tsp. salt	2 tsp. vanilla

Cream the sugar and eggs in a mixing bowl. Add the oil slowly and beat well. Sift the flour with cinnamon, salt and soda and stir into the creamed mixture, small amount at a time. Add the apples, pecans, cherries, coconut and vanilla and mix well. Pour into a greased 9-inch tube pan. Bake at 325 degrees for 1 hour.

Mrs. Calvin Stakes, Vinton, Louisiana

FRESH APPLE CAKE

2 c. sugar	2 c. chopped nuts
1 1/2 c. salad oil	1 8-oz. package cream cheese
2 eggs	1/2 stick margarine
3 c. flour	1 tsp. vanilla
1 1/2 tsp. soda	1 1-lb. box powdered sugar
1 tsp. salt	3 to 4 tbsp. milk
3 c. grated apples	

Combine the sugar, oil and eggs in a bowl and mix well. Sift the flour with soda and salt and stir into the sugar mixture. Add the apples and 1 cup nuts and beat well. Pour into 3 greased and floured 9-inch cake pans. Bake at 350 degrees for 30 to 40 minutes. Cool. Soften the cream cheese in a bowl. Add the margarine and cream well. Add the vanilla. Add powdered sugar alternately with milk and stir in remaining nuts. Spread between layers and over top and sides of cake.

Mrs. C. L. Saunders, Blooming Grove, Texas

APPLESAUCE CAKE

3 1/2 c. flour	2 c. sugar
2 tsp. soda	2 eggs
1/2 tsp. salt	2 c. seedless raisins
2 tsp. cinnamon	1 c. chopped nuts
1 tsp. cloves	1 lb. mixed candied fruits,
1/2 tsp. nutmeg	chopped
1/2 tsp. mace	2 c. hot applesauce
1 c. butter	

Sift first 7 ingredients together. Cream the butter and sugar in a bowl. Add the eggs and beat well. Mix the raisins, nuts and candied fruits with flour mixture and add to the creamed mixture alternately with the applesauce. Pour into a large tube pan. Bake at 275 degrees for 2 hours.

Mrs. L. J. Conner, Stuart, Virginia

GERMAN APPLE CAKE

1/2 c. shortening	1 tsp. baking powder
1/2 c. butter	1/4 tsp. salt
2 c. sugar	1 tsp. soda
4 eggs	1 c. cold water
3 1/2 c. flour	2 1/2 c. chopped apples
1 tsp. cinnamon	1 pkg. chopped dates
1 tsp. nutmeg	1 1/2 c. chopped walnuts
1 tsp. allspice	

Cream the shortening, butter and sugar in a mixing bowl. Add the eggs, one at a time, beating well after each addition. Sift the flour with spices, baking powder, salt and soda and add to the creamed mixture alternately with water. Stir in apples, dates and walnuts and mix thoroughly. Pour into a well-greased 9-inch tube pan. Bake at 350 degrees for 1 hour and 15 minutes.

Mrs. Jack Davis, Macon, Georgia

SALLY LUNN

1 c. scalded milk	3 eggs, beaten
1/2 c. sugar	5 c. sifted all-purpose flour
2 tsp. salt	1/2 tsp. nutmeg
1/2 c. melted butter or margarine	3 pt. fresh strawberries
1/2 c. warm water	Whipped cream
1 pkg. dry yeast	

Combine the milk, 1/4 cup sugar, salt and butter in a bowl and cool to luke-warm. Combine the water and yeast in a large mixing bowl and stir until yeast is dissolved. Add the milk mixture and eggs and mix well. Beat in the flour gradually until smooth. Cover and let rise in warm place for 1 hour or until doubled in bulk. Stir down and turn into a greased and sugared 10-inch tube pan. Cover and let rise for about 30 minutes or until doubled in bulk. Mix remaining sugar and nutmeg and sprinkle over the top. Bake in 400-degree oven for 40 minutes. Remove from oven and cool for 5 minutes. Remove from pan and mound the strawberries in the center. Serve with whipped cream. 8-10 servings.

Photograph for this recipe on page 4.

BUTTERCUP CAKE

1/2 c. shortening	1/2 tsp. salt
1 1/2 c. sugar	1 c. buttermilk
2 eggs, well beaten	1 tsp. vanilla
2 1/4 c. sifted cake flour	1/4 tsp. almond extract
1 tsp. baking powder	1/4 tsp. lemon extract
1/2 tsp. soda	1/4 tsp. orange extract

Cream the shortening in a bowl. Add sugar gradually and cream until fluffy. Blend in eggs. Sift dry ingredients together and stir into creamed mixture alternately with the buttermilk. Blend in flavorings. Pour into 2 well-greased and floured 9-inch layer pans. Bake at 350 degrees for 30 to 35 minutes.

M. G. Nussbaum, Vicksburg, Mississippi

PRINCE OF WALES CAKE

1 c. butter	3 tsp. baking powder
2 c. sugar	1/2 tsp. soda
5 eggs	1/2 tsp. salt
3 1/2 c. flour	1/2 c. molasses
1 tsp. allspice	1/2 c. buttermilk
1 tsp. cinnamon	1 pt. whipping cream
1 tsp. cloves	2 1/2 c. powdered sugar
1/2 tsp. ginger	1 box raisins, chopped

Cream the butter and sugar in a mixing bowl. Add the eggs, one at a time, beating well after each addition. Sift dry ingredients together and add to the creamed mixture alternately with the molasses and buttermilk, beginning and ending with flour mixture. Pour into 3 greased and floured 9-inch layer pans.

Bake at 325 degrees for 35 minutes. Beat the whipping cream until stiff, adding powdered sugar gradually. Fold in the raisins and spread between layers and on top of cake.

Mrs. Herbert Thomas, Sr., Wadley, Georgia

BANANA-HONEY CAKE

1 c. honey	1 1/2 c. sifted all-purpose flour
1 tsp. soda	3/4 tsp. salt
1 c. rolled oats	3/4 tsp. baking powder
3/4 c. soft butter or margarine	2 3-oz. packages soft cream cheese
1/2 c. sugar	2 1/2 c. sifted confectioners' sugar
2 eggs	
1 c. mashed bananas	

Preheat oven to 350 degrees. Pour the honey into a saucepan and bring to a boil. Add 1/2 teaspoon soda and pour over oats in a bowl. Stir and cover. Let stand for 10 minutes. Cream the butter in a large bowl. Add the sugar gradually and beat until fluffy. Blend in eggs. Add the oats mixture and bananas and beat until blended. Sift flour, remaining soda, salt and baking powder together. Add to creamed mixture and mix well. Pour into 2 greased and waxed paper-lined 8-inch round cake pans. Bake for 30 to 35 minutes and cool on a wire rack for about 10 minutes. Remove from pans and cool. Beat the cream cheese in a bowl until fluffy. Add the confectioners' sugar gradually and beat until frosting is of spreading consistency. Spread between layers and over top of cake and refrigerate. Garnish with banana slices just before serving.

DATE AND NUT PARTY CAKE

1 1/4 c. boiling water	1 /2 tsp. salt
1 c. quartered pitted dates	1 c. mayonnaise
1 c. chopped walnuts	1 c. sugar
2 c. sifted flour	1/2 oz. unsweetened chocolate
1 tsp. soda	1 tsp. vanilla
1 tsp. cinnamon	

Pour the boiling water over dates and walnuts in a bowl and set aside. Sift the flour, soda, cinnamon and salt together. Blend the mayonnaise with sugar in a mixing bowl. Melt the chocolate over hot water and stir into sugar mixture. Stir in the vanilla. Drain the date mixture and reserve water. Add sifted ingredients to mayonnaise mixture alternately with reserved water. Mix in date mixture and pour into 2 greased and waxed paper-lined 8-inch cake pans. Bake at 350 degrees for 35 minutes or until cake tests done. Cool and frost with white frosting, if desired.

MILKY WAY CAKE

8 Milky Way candy bars	4 eggs, beaten
3 sticks butter or margarine	2 1/2 c. flour
4 1/2 c. sugar	1/2 tsp. soda

1 1/4 c. buttermilk

1 c. chopped pecans

1 sm. can evaporated milk

1   6-oz. package chocolate chips

1 c. marshmallow creme

Combine candy bars and 1 stick butter in a saucepan. Cook over low heat, stirring constantly, until melted. Set aside. Cream 2 cups sugar and 1 stick butter in a bowl, then beat in eggs. Sift the flour with soda and add to the creamed mixture alternately with buttermilk. Stir in candy mixture. Add pecans and mix well. Pour into a greased and floured oblong baking pan. Bake at 325 degrees for 1 hour and 10 minutes. Combine remaining sugar, milk and remaining butter in a saucepan and cook to soft-ball stage, stirring frequently. Remove from heat and add chocolate chips and marshmallow creme. Cool slightly. Beat until thick and spread over cake.

Mrs. Earl Searls, Hurricane, West Virginia

CRANBERRY-CARROT CAKE

3 c. sifted all-purpose flour

2 tsp. baking powder

1 tsp. soda

1/2 tsp. cinnamon

1/2 tsp. nutmeg

1/2 tsp. cloves

1/2 tsp. salt

1 c. grated carrots

1 c. whole cranberry sauce

1 c. (firmly packed) light
   brown sugar

1 c. sugar

1 c. salad oil

4 eggs, well beaten

1/2 c. chopped candied lemon peel

Sift the flour, baking powder, soda, spices and salt together into a mixing bowl. Add remaining ingredients and beat with electric mixer until well blended. Pour into well-greased and floured tube pan. Bake at 350 degrees for 1 hour and 30 minutes or until top springs back when lightly touched.

Mrs. C. R. Tarpley, Fort Worth, Texas

SUPERB CHOCOLATE-KRAUT CAKE

2/3 c. butter

1 1/2 c. sugar

3 eggs, beaten

1 tsp. vanilla

1/2 c. cocoa

2 1/4 c. flour

1 tsp. baking powder

1/4 tsp. salt

1 c. water

2/3 c. chopped sauerkraut, drained

Cream the butter and sugar in a bowl and beat in eggs and vanilla. Sift the cocoa, flour, baking powder and salt together and add to the creamed mixture alternately with water. Fold in the sauerkraut and pour into 2 greased and floured layer pans. Bake at 350 degrees for 25 to 30 minutes. Frost with coconut-almond frosting.

Mrs. James I. Ulls, Blacksburg, Virginia

GERMAN CHOCOLATE CAKE

1 4-oz. bar sweet cooking chocolate	1 tsp. vanilla
1/2 c. boiling water	2 1/2 c. sifted cake flour
1 c. butter or margarine	1/2 tsp. salt
2 c. sugar	1 tsp. soda
4 eggs, separated	1 c. buttermilk

Melt the chocolate in the boiling water and cool. Cream the butter and sugar in a bowl until fluffy. Add the egg yolks, one at a time, mixing well after each addition. Add the chocolate and vanilla and mix well. Sift flour, salt and soda together and add to chocolate mixture alternately with buttermilk. Beat until smooth. Fold in stiffly beaten egg whites and pour into 3 greased and waxed paper-lined 8 or 9-inch layer pans. Bake at 350 degrees for 30 to 40 minutes. Cool for 10 minutes, then remove from pans.

Coconut-Pecan Frosting

1 c. evaporated milk	1 tsp. vanilla
1 c. sugar	1 1/3 c. flaked coconut
3 egg yolks	1 c. chopped pecans
1/2 c. butter or margarine	

Combine first 5 ingredients in a saucepan and cook and stir over medium heat for about 12 minutes or until thickened. Add the coconut and pecans and beat until thick enough to spread. Frost cake.

Mrs. Lawrence Randolph, Bear Creek, Alabama

CUERO CAKE

1 c. butter	1/2 c. orange juice
2 1/2 c. sugar	1 tsp. vanilla
5 eggs, separated	1 tsp. soda
2 sq. chocolate, melted	1 c. buttermilk
Grated rind of 1 orange	3 c. sifted cake flour

Cream the butter in a bowl and add sugar gradually. Add beaten egg yolks and mix well. Add the chocolate, grated rind, orange juice and vanilla and mix well. Mix the soda with buttermilk and add to the creamed mixture alternately with flour. Beat well. Fold in stiffly beaten egg whites and pour into 3 greased and waxed paper-lined 9-inch cake pans. Bake at 350 degrees for about 30 minutes or until cake tests done.

Filling

1 sm. can crushed pineapple	1 tbsp. butter
2 eggs, beaten	1 tbsp. lemon juice
1 c. sugar	1 c. shredded coconut
3 tbsp. flour	

Mix first 4 ingredients in top of double boiler. Cook over boiling water, stirring constantly, until thickened. Remove from heat. Add the butter, lemon juice and coconut and mix well. Cool. Spread between cake layers. Ice the top and sides of cake with Seven-Minute icing.

Mrs. Joalice Poehler, Big Lake, Texas

FINNISH CAKE

1 pkg. sweet cooking chocolate	1 tsp. baking powder
1/2 c. shortening	1/2 tsp. salt
2 sticks butter	1 c. milk
3 c. sugar	1 c. chopped almonds
5 eggs	Vanilla ice cream
1tsp. lemon flavoring	Apricot halves
1 tsp. vanilla	Almonds
3 c. flour	Chocolate curls

Melt the chocolate over hot water. Cream the shortening and butter in a large mixing bowl. Add the sugar gradually and cream well. Add the eggs, one at a time, beating well after each addition, then stir in the flavorings. Sift the flour, baking powder and salt together and add to the sugar mixture alternately with milk. Stir in the almonds and pour into a greased large ring mold or bundt pan. Bake at 350 degrees for 1 hour and 15 minutes. Cool for 10 minutes and remove from mold. Cool. Place on a cake plate. Fill center of cake with ice cream and garnish with apricots, almonds and chocolate curls.

Photograph for this recipe on page 10.

BROWNSTONE FRONT CAKE

2 sticks butter or margarine	1 tsp. soda
2 c. sugar	1/4 tsp. salt
3 eggs, separated	1 c. buttermilk
2 sq. chocolate, melted	3 c. sifted flour

Cream the butter and sugar in a mixing bowl. Add egg yolks and chocolate and beat well. Dissolve the soda and salt in buttermilk and add to the creamed mixture alternately with flour. Fold in the beaten egg whites. Pour into 3 greased and floured layer pans. Bake at 350 degrees for about 45 minutes.

Icing

2 sticks butter	1 c. evaporated milk
2 c. sugar	1 tsp. vanilla

Combine the butter, sugar and milk in a saucepan and mix well. Place over low heat and bring to boiling point. Reduce heat and simmer for 45 minutes. Cool. Add vanilla and beat until thick. Spread between layers and on top and side of cake.

Mrs. Hampton Scruggs, Brevard, North Carolina

RED VELVET CAKE

1 1/2 c. sugar	1 tsp. salt
2 c. salad oil	2 tbsp. cocoa
2 eggs, beaten	1 c. buttermilk
1 tsp. vinegar	2 tsp. vanilla
1 2-oz. bottle red food coloring	1 stick margarine
	1 8-oz. package cream cheese
2 1/2 c. flour	1 box powdered sugar
1 tsp. soda	1 c. chopped nuts

Cream the sugar and oil in a mixing bowl. Add eggs and beat well. Add the vinegar and food coloring and beat well. Sift the flour, soda, salt and cocoa together and add to the creamed mixture alternately with buttermilk. Add 1 teaspoon vanilla and beat well. Pour into 2 greased and floured cake pans. Bake at 350 degrees for 30 to 35 minutes. Cream the margarine and cream cheese in a bowl and add remaining vanilla. Sift the powdered sugar and add to the creamed mixture gradually. Add nuts and mix well. Spread on top of cake layers and place layers together. Spread on side of cake.

Barbara Love, Albany, Georgia

TOASTED COCONUT CAKE

1 1/4 c. boiling water	1 tsp. salt
1 c. quick-cooking oats	1 tsp. baking powder
1 c. sugar	1 tsp. soda
1 c. (packed) brown sugar	1 1/2 tsp. cinnamon
1/2 c. oil	1 1/2 to 2 c. flour
2 eggs, beaten	1 tsp. vanilla

Pour boiling water over the oats and let stand for 20 minutes. Cream the sugars and oil in a bowl and stir in eggs and oatmeal. Sift salt, baking powder, soda, cinnamon and flour together and stir into creamed mixture. Add vanilla and pour into a greased oblong baking pan. Bake at 350 degrees until cake tests done. Cool for 5 minutes.

Topping

6 tbsp. melted butter or margarine	1 tsp. vanilla
	1 c. shredded coconut
3 tbsp. milk	1/4 c. chopped nuts (opt.)
1 3/4 c. (packed) brown sugar	

Mix all ingredients and spread over cake. Broil until lightly browned.

Mrs. Robert E. Davy, Junction, West Virginia

SOUR CREAM CAKE

3 c. sugar	1/2 pt. sour cream
1 c. shortening or margarine	1 tsp. vanilla
6 eggs, separated	1 tsp. lemon extract

| 1 tsp. butter flavoring | 1/2 tsp. salt |
| 1/4 tsp. soda | 3 c. flour |

Cream the sugar and shortening in a bowl and add egg yolks, one at a time. Add the sour cream and flavorings and beat well. Add remaining ingredients and beat for 5 minutes. Fold in stiffly beaten egg whites. Pour into a greased and floured tube pan. Bake at 300 degrees for 1 hour and 30 minutes. Cool in pan for 5 minutes, then remove from pan.

Nola E. Koonce, Florence, Alabama

GINGERBREAD WITH HARD SAUCE

1/2 c. butter	1 tsp. salt
1 c. sugar	2 tsp. ginger
1 c. dark molasses	2 tsp. cinnamon
2 eggs, separated	1 c. buttermilk
3 c. sifted cake flour	Hard Sauce
1 tsp. soda	

Cream the butter in a bowl. Add sugar and cream until light and smooth. Add the molasses and beaten egg yolks and mix thoroughly. Sift the flour with soda, salt and spices and add to creamed mixture alternately with buttermilk. Fold in stiffly beaten egg whites and turn into well-greased and floured mold. Bake at 350 degrees for 30 to 40 minutes. Serve hot topped with Hard Sauce.

Hard Sauce

| 1/2 c. butter | 1 egg, separated |
| 1 1/2 c. sifted confectioners' sugar | 2 tsp. grated lemon rind |

Cream the butter and sugar in bowl and add the egg yolk, beating constantly. Blend in lemon rind and fold in stiffly beaten egg white. Chill.

WHIPPED CREAM CAKE

1 c. heavy cream
1 c. sugar
2 eggs, beaten
1 tsp. vanilla

1 1/2 c. cake flour
2 tsp. baking powder
Pinch of salt

Whip the heavy cream until slightly thickened and fold in the sugar. Fold in eggs and vanilla. Sift the flour with the baking powder and salt and fold into the cream mixture. Place in 2 greased layer pans or 1 loaf pan. Bake in 350-degree oven for 25 minutes and cool. Fill and frost with Seven-Minute icing.

Vergie Kahla, Port Bolivar Texas

CRANBERRY CAKE

2 1/4 c. flour
1 tsp. baking powder
1 tsp. soda
1/4 tsp. salt
1 c. sugar
3/4 c. shortening
2 eggs

1 c. buttermilk
2 tbsp. orange juice
1 tbsp. grated orange rind
1 c. chopped fresh cranberries
1 c. chopped dates
1 c. chopped nuts

Sift the flour with baking powder, soda and salt. Cream the sugar, shortening and eggs in a mixing bowl, then add the sifted ingredients alternately with buttermilk. Add the orange juice, grated peel, cranberries, dates and nuts and mix well. Pour into a greased and floured loaf pan. Bake at 350 degrees for 1 hour and leave in pan.

Glaze

1 c. powdered sugar

1/2 c. orange juice

Mix the powdered sugar and orange juice and pour over warm cake. Cool the cake and remove from pan. Wrap in foil and refrigerate for 24 hours.

Mrs. Guy H. Smith, McCoy, Texas

GRAHAM CRACKER-NUT CAKE

1 1/2 c. sugar
2 sticks butter or margarine
6 eggs
1 lb. graham crackers, crushed

1 c. milk
1/2 tsp. vanilla
1 lb. dates, chopped
3 c. broken pecans

Cream the sugar and butter in a mixing bowl. Add the eggs, one at a time, beating well after each addition. Add cracker crumbs, milk, vanilla, dates and pecans and mix well. Spread in a greased shallow baking pan. Bake at 350 degrees until cake tests done and cut in squares.

Mrs. C. L. DeVane, Plant City, Florida

ENGLISH FILBERT FRUIT CAKE

1 c. butter or margarine
2 c. (firmly packed) dark brown
   sugar
6 eggs
1/2 c. currant jelly
1/2 c. molasses
Grated peel and juice of 1 orange
Grated peel and juice of 1 lemon
3 c. sifted all-purpose flour
1 tsp. baking powder
1 tsp. salt
1 tsp. cinnamon

1 tsp. nutmeg
1/2 tsp. mace
1/2 tsp. cloves
1/2 tsp. soda
3/4 c. cognac
1 lb. dark seedless raisins
1 lb. mixed candied fruits
1/2 lb. chopped dates
1/2 lb. golden seedless raisins
1/2 lb. toasted chopped filberts
Cognac Glaze
Halved filberts

Cream the butter and sugar in a bowl until fluffy and beat in eggs, one at a time. Blend in the jelly, molasses, orange peel, orange juice, lemon peel and lemon juice. Sift the flour, baking powder, salt, spices and soda together and add to creamed mixture alternately with cognac. Combine the fruits and chopped filberts and stir into flour mixture. Turn into a greased and foil-lined 10-inch tube pan. Bake in 300-degree oven for about 3 hours and 30 minutes or until cake tests done. Cover with foil during last hour of baking to prevent burning, if necessary. Cool thoroughly in pan. Remove from pan and wrap in cognac-soaked cheesecloth, then in foil. Store in an airtight container for several weeks to mellow, soaking cloth-wrapped cake with additional cognac, if desired. Frost top of cake with Cognac Glaze and top with filbert halves just before serving.

Cognac Glaze

2 tbsp. cognac
2 to 3 tsp. water

1 1/2 c. sifted confectioners'
   sugar

Blend the cognac and water with confectioners' sugar in a bowl.

JAPANESE FRUITCAKE

3 c. flour	1 c. chopped nuts
1 tsp. cinnamon	1 c. butter
1 tsp. allspice	2 c. sugar
1 tsp. nutmeg	4 eggs
1 tsp. cloves	1 c. milk
1 tsp. baking powder	1 c. jam
1 c. seedless raisins	

Sift 2 cups flour with spices and baking powder. Mix remaining flour with raisins and nuts. Cream the butter and sugar in a mixing bowl and add eggs, one at a time. Add the spice mixture alternately with milk. Add jam and nut mixture and mix well. Pour into 3 greased cake pans. Bake at 350 degrees for 35 minutes.

Frosting

2 c. flaked coconut	1 sm. can crushed pineapple
Grated rind of 3 oranges	2 1/2 c. sugar
Juice of 3 oranges	2 tbsp. flour

Combine all ingredients in a saucepan and mix well. Cook until thick, stirring constantly, then cool. Spread between layers and on top and side of cake.

Mrs. Travis Oswalt, Russellville, Alabama

LADY BALTIMORE CAKE

3/4 c. butter	1 c. milk
2 c. sugar	1 tsp. lemon flavoring
3 1/2 tsp. baking powder	8 egg whites, stiffly beaten
3 1/2 c. flour	

Cream the butter in a bowl and add sugar gradually. Sift the baking powder and flour together 3 times and add to the creamed mixture alternately with milk. Add lemon flavoring and fold in egg whites. Pour into 3 greased and floured layer pans. Bake at 350 degrees until cake tests done.

Icing

3 c. sugar	1 c. chopped raisins
1 c. boiling water	1/2 c. chopped candied cherries
3 egg whites, stiffly beaten	1 c. chopped nuts
1 c. chopped citron	1 tsp. lemon flavoring

Combine the sugar and water in a saucepan and stir until sugar is dissolved. Bring to a boil and cook, without stirring, until syrup spins a thread. Pour over egg whites slowly, beating constantly. Beat until stiff. Add fruits, nuts and lemon flavoring and spread on cake layers. Place layers together and spread icing over top and side of cake.

Mrs. R. E. Chappell, Dothan, Alabama

WHITE FRUITCAKE

1 1/2 c. pineapple chunks	2 tsp. baking powder
1 c. chopped citron	2 tsp. salt
1 c. candied cherries	4 c. sifted flour
1 c. golden seedless raisins	3/4 c. shortening
1 c. chopped candied lemon rind	1/4 c. margarine
1 c. chopped candied orange rind	2 c. sugar
1 c. chopped almonds	8 eggs, separated
1 1/2 c. walnut halves	3/4 c. milk

Combine fruits and nuts. Sift the baking powder, salt and flour together and stir in nut mixture. Cream the shortening, margarine and sugar until fluffy. Add egg yolks and mix well. Stir in the flour mixture alternately with milk and fold in stiffly beaten egg whites. Spoon into 3 greased and brown paper-lined loaf pans. Bake at 300 degrees for about 2 hours and 30 minutes or until top is firm when lightly touched. Bake at 275 degrees if baking dish is used.

Mrs. O. E. Wood, Dryden, Virginia

STRAWBERRY JAM CAKE

3 c. sugar	1 c. milk
1 c. strawberry jam	1 lge. can crushed pineapple
2 c. flour	Grated rind of 1 orange
3/4 c. soft butter	1/4 apple, diced
1/2 c. buttermilk	1 can shredded coconut
1 tsp. soda	1 c. chopped nuts
3 eggs	

Place 1 cup sugar, jam, flour, butter, buttermilk, soda and eggs in a large mixing bowl. Beat with an electric mixer at high speed for 5 minutes. Pour into 2 greased and floured 9-inch layer pans. Bake at 325 degrees for 40 minutes or until cake tests done. Mix remaining sugar and milk in a saucepan and cook to soft-ball stage. Remove from heat and add remaining ingredients. Cool and beat until thick. Spread on cake layers and place layers together.

Mrs. Gayle Goff, Humboldt, Tennessee

LEMON-NUT CAKE

2 c. butter	1 tsp. baking powder
2 c. sugar	1 lb. white seedless raisins
6 eggs	5 c. chopped pecans
4 c. flour	1 2-oz. bottle lemon extract

Cream the butter and sugar in a mixing bowl. Add the eggs, one at a time, beating well after each addition. Sift flour and baking powder together. Add the raisins and pecans and mix until coated. Add to the creamed mixture gradually. Add the lemon extract and mix well. Pour into a tube pan. Bake at 300 degrees for 30 minutes. Reduce temperature to 275 degrees and bake for 1 hour longer. One cup chopped candied cherries may be substituted for 1 cup pecans.

Mrs. A. Henderson, Jackson, Mississippi

BLACK WALNUT CAKE

1 c. butter	1 tsp. vanilla
2 c. sugar	1 c. milk
3 c. flour	1 c. chopped black walnuts
2 1/2 tsp. baking powder	4 eggs
1 tsp. salt	

Cream the butter and sugar in a mixing bowl. Sift the flour, baking powder and salt together and stir into creamed mixture. Stir in the vanilla and milk. Add the black walnuts, then eggs and mix well. Pour into 3 greased and floured 9-inch round cake pans. Bake at 375 degrees until cake tests done.

White Fudge Frosting

3 c. sugar	1 tsp. vanilla
1 c. milk	1 c. chopped black walnuts
1 stick butter	

Combine the sugar and milk in a saucepan and bring to a boil. Cover the saucepan. Cook for 5 minutes, remove from heat and add butter and vanilla. Cool. Beat until thickened. Spread on cake and sprinkle walnuts between layers and on top of cake.

Mrs. Joe L. Richardson, Walhalla, South Carolina

PEANUT CAKE

3/4 c. butter	4 tsp. baking powder
2 c. sugar	1/2 c. milk
4 eggs, separated	1 c. chopped peanuts
3 1/2 c. all-purpose flour	1 tsp. vanilla

Cream the butter in a bowl and add sugar gradually. Add the egg yolks and beat thoroughly. Sift flour and baking powder together and add to the creamed mixture alternately with milk. Add peanuts and beat well. Fold in the stiffly beaten egg whites and vanilla and pour into a loaf pan. Bake at 350 degrees for 40 to 50 minutes or until done.

Clara Burton, Chandlerville, Kentucky

TOASTED BUTTER-PECAN CAKE

2 c. chopped pecans	2 c. sugar
1 1/4 c. butter	4 eggs
3 c. flour	1 c. milk
2 tsp. baking powder	2 tsp. vanilla
1/2 tsp. salt	

Preheat oven to 350 degrees. Place the pecans and 1/4 cup butter in a shallow baking pan. Bake for 20 to 25 minutes or until pecans are toasted, stirring frequently. Sift flour with baking powder and salt. Cream remaining butter in a bowl and add sugar gradually, creaming well. Add the eggs, one at a time, beating well after each addition. Add sifted ingredients alternately with milk, beginning and ending with sifted ingredients. Stir in vanilla and 1 1/3 cups pecans and pour into 3 greased and floured 8-inch round layer pans. Bake at 350 degrees for 25 to 30 minutes. Cool.

Butter-Pecan Frosting:

1/4 c. butter	**1 tsp. vanilla**
1 lb. sifted powdered sugar	**4 to 6 tbsp. evaporated milk**

Cream the butter in a bowl and add powdered sugar, vanilla and enough evaporated milk until of spreading consistency. Stir in remaining pecans and frost cake.

Mrs. John Cannon, Draper, North Carolina

POUND CAKE

3 1/2 c. sifted cake flour	**1 lb. confectioners' sugar**
1 tsp. baking powder	**8 eggs**
1/2 tsp. salt	**1 tsp. vanilla**
1/4 tsp. mace	**1/2 tsp. almond extract**
1 3/4 c. butter	**1/2 tsp. lemon extract**

Preheat oven to 325 degrees. Combine the flour with baking powder, salt and mace and sift together 2 times. Cream butter in a bowl until light and fluffy. Add the sugar slowly and beat until mixture resembles whipped cream. Add the eggs, one at a time, beating well after each addition. Stir in half the flour mixture, then add flavorings and remaining flour mixture. Pour into greased 10 x 4-inch tube pan and cut through batter several times with knife to break air bubbles. Bake for 1 hour to 1 hour and 10 minutes. Remove from pan immediately and cool on cake rack. Dust with additional confectioners' sugar.

BROWN SUGAR POUND CAKE

2 sticks butter	3 1/2 c. cake flour
1/2 c. shortening	1/2 tsp. baking powder
1 1-lb. box brown sugar	1 c. milk
1 c. sugar	1 1/2 tsp. vanilla
5 eggs	

Cream the butter and shortening in a bowl and add the sugars, 1 cup at a time. Add the eggs, one at a time, beating well after each addition. Sift flour and baking powder together and add to the creamed mixture alternately with milk. Add the vanilla and mix well. Pour into a tube pan. Bake at 360 degrees for 2 hours.

Icing

3 c. sugar	1 stick margarine
1/2 c. water	1 tsp. vinegar
1 egg, beaten	Pinch of salt
1 c. milk	

Place 1/2 cup sugar in a heavy skillet. Cook over low heat, stirring constantly, until melted and brown. Add the water and stir until dissolved. Add remaining sugar. Mix the egg with milk and stir into sugar mixture. Add margarine, vinegar and salt. Cook to soft-ball stage and cool. Beat until creamy and spread on cake.

Mrs. Maude B. Fordham, Cochran, Georgia

SOUR CREAM POUND CAKE

3 c. sifted cake flour	2 sticks margarine, softened
1/4 tsp. soda	3 c. sugar
1/2 tsp. salt	1 tsp. vanilla
6 eggs, separated	1 8-oz. carton sour cream

Preheat oven to 350 degrees. Sift the flour and soda together 3 times. Add 1/4 teaspoon salt to egg whites and beat until stiff peaks form. Cream the margarine and sugar in a bowl and add remaining salt and vanilla. Add the egg yolks, one at a time, beating well after each addition. Add the flour mixture alternately with sour cream, beginning and ending with flour mixture. Fold in egg whites and pour into a greased and floured 10-inch tube pan. Bake for 1 hour or until cake tests done. Cool on rack.

Cream Cheese Frosting

1 8-oz. package cream cheese	Evaporated milk
1 stick margarine	1 tsp. vanilla
1 1-lb. box confectioners' sugar	1 c. broken pecans

Soften the cream cheese and margarine. Place in a mixing bowl and cream well. Mix in the sugar gradually and add enough milk for spreading consistency. Add vanilla and pecans and mix well. Spread on cake.

Joy Miles, Florence, Alabama

STRAWBERRY-RUM CAKE

1/2 c. sugar	1 1-lb. 1-oz. package pound
1 c. water	cake mix
1 c. rum	Sweetened whipped cream
2 pt. fresh strawberries	

Dissolve the sugar in water in a saucepan over low heat. Remove from heat and stir in rum. Reserve 1 cup whole strawberries. Halve remaining strawberries and add to rum syrup. Let stand for at least 1 hour. Prepare cake mix according to package directions and pour into ungreased 9-inch ring mold. Bake at 325 degrees for 1 hour or until golden brown and cake tests done. Loosen edges with spatula carefully and turn out onto serving platter. Drain the halved strawberries and reserve syrup. Pour reserved syrup over entire surface of cake slowly until all is absorbed and cool. Heap strawberry halves in center of ring and top with whipped cream. Garnish with reserved whole strawberries and serve.

PEACH UPSIDE-DOWN CAKE

1/4 c. soft butter or margarine	1 egg
1/2 c. (packed) brown sugar	1 1/4 c. sifted cake flour
1 1/2 c. drained canned	1 1/2 tsp. baking powder
sliced peaches	1/2 tsp. salt
6 maraschino cherries, halved	1/2 tsp. grated orange rind
1/3 c. shortening	1/2 c. orange juice
1/2 c. sugar	

Spread butter in bottom of 8-inch round cake pan and sprinkle with brown sugar. Arrange peaches and cherries on brown sugar. Cream the shortening and sugar in a bowl. Add the egg and beat well. Sift the flour, baking powder and salt together and add to creamed mixture alternately with mixture of orange rind and juice. Pour over peaches carefully. Bake at 350 degrees for 45 to 50 minutes or until cake tests done. Cool for 10 minutes. Invert over serving plate and remove cake from cake pan. 6-8 servings.

Mrs. Onice Keel, Slocomb, Alabama

BROWN SUGAR FROSTING

3 c. (firmly packed) brown sugar   1/4 c. butter or margarine
1 1/8 c. light cream   Vanilla to taste

Combine the brown sugar and cream in a saucepan and cook over low heat to soft-ball stage. Remove from heat. Add butter and cool. Add vanilla and beat until frosting is of spreading consistency. Frost cooled cake.

CARAMEL FROSTING

3 c. sugar   2 tbsp. light corn syrup
1/4 c. boiling water   1/4 tsp. soda
1/2 c. milk   1 tsp. vanilla
1/2 c. butter

Melt 1/4 cup sugar in a heavy skillet, stirring constantly. Add boiling water and stir until dissolved. Combine remaining ingredients except vanilla in a large saucepan and stir in sugar syrup. Cook to soft-ball stage and remove from heat. Cool. Beat to spreading consistency and add vanilla. Add several drops of boiling water, if needed, to spread.

Mrs. Edwin F. Cook, Blairsville, Georgia

MAGIC CARAMEL ICING

2 c. sugar   1 c. shortening
1 c. buttermilk   1 tsp. soda

Combine all ingredients in a 4-quart saucepan and mix well. Cook to soft-ball stage, stirring constantly, and remove from heat. Beat until creamy and thick enough to spread. One-half cup margarine may be substituted for half the shortening.

Mrs. Benny Teague, Chewalla, Tennessee

CARAMEL-BUTTERMILK ICING

1/4 lb. butter or margarine	1/2 tsp. soda
2 c. sugar	1 tbsp. light corn syrup
1/2 c. buttermilk	Pinch of salt

Combine all ingredients in a saucepan. Cook over low heat, stirring constantly, to soft-ball stage and remove from heat. Beat until thick enough to spread. Icing for 2 layers.

Mrs. S. N. Kitchens, Moulton, Alabama

LEMON FLUFF FROSTING

1/2 c. margarine	3 tbsp. lemon juice
Dash of salt	2 tsp. grated lemon peel
4 c. sifted confectioners' sugar	

Cream the margarine in a bowl. Add the salt and half the sugar and cream well. Add remaining sugar alternately with lemon juice and cream until light and fluffy. Add lemon peel and mix thoroughly.

FLUFFY ORANGE FROSTING

2 egg whites
1 1/2 c. sugar
1/2 tsp. cream of tartar

1/2 c. orange juice
1 tsp. vanilla
1/8 tsp. yellow food coloring

Place all ingredients in top of a double boiler and place over boiling water. Beat with electric mixer at high speed for 5 to 7 minutes or until mixture stands in peaks. Remove from boiling water. Beat until thick and spread on sides and top of cake.

SOUR CREAM VELVET FROSTING

1 6-oz. package semisweet
   chocolate pieces
1/2 c. butter or margarine
1/2 c. sour cream

1/2 tsp. vanilla
1/2 tsp. almond flavoring
1/4 tsp. salt
1 1-lb. box powdered sugar

Melt the chocolate pieces and butter in a heatproof bowl over hot water. Remove from heat and blend in sour cream, flavorings and salt. Beat in enough sugar gradually until frosting is of spreading consistency. Frosting for 2 layers or 1 tube cake.

Ethel Johnston, Dallas, Texas

CHOCOLATE FROSTING

4 sq. unsweetened chocolate
1 stick butter, softened
2 eggs

1 box powdered sugar
4 tbsp. hot water
2 tsp. vanilla

Melt the chocolate in a heatproof bowl over hot water. Add remaining ingredients and place bowl in ice. Beat until creamy and spread on cake.

Ruth Crews, Thomasville, North Carolina

BROWN SUGAR-COCOA ICING

2 c. (packed) brown sugar
4 tbsp. cocoa
4 tbsp. milk
1 tsp. vanilla

1/4 lb. butter, softened
1 c. chopped nuts (opt.)
1 tsp. baking powder

Mix all ingredients except the baking powder in a saucepan and bring to a boil. Cook for 1 minute, stirring constantly. Remove from heat, add baking powder and beat to spreading consistency.

Mrs. Sam Pruitt, Manchester, Georgia

GROUND PECAN FROSTING

3 tbsp. light corn syrup
1 1/2 c. water
1 1/2 c. sugar

4 egg whites, stiffly beaten
3 c. ground pecans

Mix the corn syrup, water and sugar in a saucepan and cook until mixture spins a thread. Pour over egg whites slowly, beating constantly until thick. Frosting for 3 layers.

Mrs. W. W. Lowery, Trenton, North Carolina

DIVINITY ICING

2 c. sugar
1/2 c. cold water
1 tbsp. salad oil

1 tsp. vinegar
2 egg whites
Pinch of salt

Combine first 4 ingredients in a saucepan and cook until syrup spins a thread. Beat the egg whites and salt in a mixing bowl with electric mixer at high speed until stiff peaks form. Add the hot syrup slowly, beating constantly with mixer at low speed. Beat for 3 minutes longer or until thick enough to spread.

Mrs. Ova Amyx, Grassy Creek, Kentucky

FUDGY WHITE FROSTING

2 1/2 tbsp. flour
1/2 c. milk
1/2 c. shortening
1/2 c. sugar

1/2 tsp. vanilla or almond
    flavoring
Dash of salt
3 to 3 1/2 c. powdered sugar

Combine the flour and milk in a saucepan and cook over low heat until thick, stirring constantly. Cool. Combine the shortening, sugar, vanilla and salt in a bowl and beat with mixer until fluffy. Add the flour mixture and beat for 1 minute longer. Beat in enough of the powdered sugar for spreading consistency. Frosting for 2 layers.

Mrs. W. T. Parker, Jr., Crestview, Florida

ALMOND CREAM FILLING

1/4 c. flour	1/2 c. confectioners' sugar
1/4 c. sugar	2 tsp. vanilla
1 1/4 c. milk	1/2 c. slivered almonds
Butter or margarine	

Combine the flour, sugar and 1/4 cup milk and mix well. Scald remaining milk in a saucepan and stir in flour mixture slowly. Cook, stirring constantly, for about 5 minutes or until thick and remove from heat. Cool until lukewarm. Cream 1/2 cup butter, confectioners' sugar and vanilla and stir into cooled mixture. Brown the almonds in 1 tablespoon butter in a skillet, stirring constantly. Stir into filling and chill until firm enough to spread.

Irene H. Nelson, Talladega, Alabama

HONEY-ORANGE FILLING

1 tbsp. flour	1/4 c. orange juice
2 tbsp. cornstarch	2 tbsp. water
1/2 c. honey	1 tbsp. lemon juice
1 tsp. salt	1 tsp. butter
2 egg yolks	Grated rind of 1 orange

Mix the flour, cornstarch, honey, salt and egg yolks in top of a double boiler. Mix the orange juice, water and lemon juice and add to flour mixture slowly. Add the butter and orange rind. Cook over boiling water, stirring, until thickened. Cool and spread between cake layers.

Georgia N. Watson, Blossom, Texas

LEMON CHEESE FILLING

1 c. sugar	Grated rind of 2 lemons
1/2 c. butter or margarine	2 eggs, well beaten
Juice of 2 lemons	

Combine the sugar, butter, lemon juice and grated rind in top of a double boiler and cook over boiling water until sugar is dissolved, stirring frequently. Remove from boiling water and stir into eggs. Return to double boiler and cook until mixture coats spoon, stirring constantly.

Mrs. Berry Floyd, Canon, Georgia

HEAVENLY LEMON FILLING

8 egg yolks, slightly beaten	2 tbsp. grated lemon rind
1 c. sugar	1/4 tsp. salt
6 tbsp. lemon juice	1 pt. heavy cream

Place the egg yolks in top of a double boiler and stir in sugar, lemon juice, lemon rind and salt. Cook over boiling water for about 10 minutes or until thick, stirring frequently. Cool. Whip cream until thick and fold into lemon mixture. Cover. Refrigerate until chilled.

Mrs. Charlene Broome Strickland, Danielsville, Georgia

DELICIOUS LEMON CHEESE FILLING

6 lge. egg yolks, well beaten
2 c. sugar
Juice of 2 lemons

Grated rind of 2 lemons
1/4 c. butter
2 tbsp. confectioners' sugar (opt.)

Mix the egg yolks, sugar, lemon juice, grated rind and butter in top of a double boiler and cook over boiling water until thickened, stirring frequently. Cool and add confectioners' sugar.

Claire S. Chester, Camp Hill, Alabama

FRUIT FILLING FOR CAKE

1 c. drained crushed pineapple
1 c. cooked dried apricots
1/2 c. sugar

3 tbsp. orange juice
1 tbsp. grated orange rind
1 c. flaked coconut

Combine the pineapple, apricots and sugar in a saucepan and cook until thick, stirring constantly. Stir in orange juice, orange rind and coconut and cool. Spread between cake layers.

Mrs. J. M. Isbell, Rossville, Georgia

RHUBARB FILLING

1/2 lb. fresh rhubarb
5/8 c. sugar
2 tbsp. water
2 tbsp. cornstarch

1/4 tsp. salt
1/2 tsp. grated lemon rind
1 tsp. lemon juice

Wash the rhubarb and cut into 1/2-inch pieces. Cook with 1/2 cup sugar and water in a saucepan for about 15 minutes or until soft. Combine remaining sugar, cornstarch and salt in a small saucepan and stir in rhubarb mixture. Cook and stir over low heat until thickened and clear. Add lemon rind and lemon juice and cool.

meringues, tortes, & cheesecakes

Lavish . . . elegant . . . very special . . . these words and more describe meringues, tortes, and cheesecakes. These desserts add excitement to any meal with their eye-stopping beauty and smooth, rich taste.

They carry an extra bonus for today's nutrition-conscious homemaker — they are rich in much-needed protein derived from their cheese-and-eggs foundation. How marvelous that something so beautiful is also good for you!

Southern homemakers number meringues, tortes, and cheesecakes among their very favorite desserts — as evidenced by the wonderfully varied collection of recipes in the following pages. These are the recipes southern homemakers turn to when they want to serve an extra-special dessert to impress both family and guests. Every one of these recipes has passed that most critical of all tests — it has won the approval of family and friends.

Now you too can share in the rich bounty of these homemakers' cooking skills. Every recipe in this exciting section has been carefully prepared to achieve just the right balance of flavors, textures, and ingredients. With these recipes, you can win words of praise from your family and guests.

The next time you want to mark an occasion as extra-special, prepare a torte, meringue, or cheesecake for the dessert. People will get your message — and you'll get their compliments.

Some desserts look so elegant and taste so delightful, they turn an ordinary meal into a festive occasion. Certainly this is true of meringues, tortes, and cheesecakes. These desserts are the standard of fine dining. In fact, many restaurants, such as Lindy's in New York, have built fabulous reputations around such marvelous desserts.

Don't be reluctant to try your hand at these desserts. For all their fragile appearance and marvelous flavor, meringues, tortes, and cheesecakes are surprisingly easy to make.

Cheesecakes are very rich, sweet, and creamy cakes made from various cheese preparations — cottage cheese, sweetened cheese curds, or cream cheese combined with eggs, milk, and flavorings. Fruit juices or rind, nuts, and other condiments are often added to cheesecake batters for special

cooking methods

FOR MERINGUES, TORTES, AND CHEESECAKES

flavor and texture. Many cheesecakes are baked in a crust made of sweet cracker crumbs.

Almost all cheesecakes — except those which are baked in a pie shell — should be cooked in a spring-form pan. These pans have sides that come away from the cake, leaving it sitting on the bottom of the pan. They are used because this cake is delicate and must be carefully handled.

When baking your cheesecake, watch the oven temperature carefully. These desserts usually cook at low heat and they are often left to cool in an opened, turned-off oven. You should expect a slight degree of shrinkage. However, if there is much shrinkage, the cake was baked at too high a temperature.

Cheesecakes should be chilled thoroughly — for about 12 hours — before serving. If you want to dress it up, try shaving chocolate curls onto the top or preparing one of the ever-popular fruit toppings — strawberry, blueberry, apricot, or cherry.

Store your cheesecake in the refrigerator. Eggs and cheese form the base for this dessert, so it is highly susceptible to bacterial activity. If not properly stored, it will not be safe to eat, even though it may not look spoiled.

Tortes are the classic German dessert — very rich sponge-like cakes which sometimes contain finely ground nuts and bread crumbs in place of flour. Nuts for a torte should never be ground in an ordinary meat grinder, as this will crush the nuts rather than grind them and will bring up oil. A small hand grinder will yield the fluffy, light, dry particles needed for a perfect torte.

Another good rule for making tortes is to never grease the pan. Because tortes are basically a kind of sponge cake, they depend upon the clinging of the batter to the sides of the pan for levening action. If the sides are greased, the batter cannot rise. Like cheesecakes, tortes should be baked in a spring-form pan because they are too delicate to stand much handling. Tortes should be stored in the refrigerator until serving time.

Tortes are elegantly delicious served without topping in traditional German fashion. If your family has a real sweet tooth, try icing the torte very lightly or garnishing it with sweetened whipped cream or a delightfully tart fruit sauce.

Meringues are another delicious and elegant dessert. For many people, the word "meringue" brings to mind the delicately-browned topping of a lemon meringue pie. But in this section, "meringue" refers to a small baked shell made of whipped egg whites and sugar. These air-light creations are most often filled with one of the many custard fillings. Some people enjoy them filled with fresh fruit while others prefer the meringue with just a touch of sweetened whipped cream. Whatever your preference, if your menu calls for a heavy and filling main course, meringues could be just the finishing touch you need.

The lightness of meringues results from the reaction of egg whites to baking. Egg whites are almost pure albumin, a substance which is able to hold the air beaten into it and to stretch as that air expands, as it will during baking.

When sugar is added to *beaten* egg whites, it increases the amount of air the whites can hold. And when sugar is added to *unbeaten* egg whites and the two are beaten together, not only is the amount of air increased, but the meringue can hold that air very much longer. The importance of using the proper method in preparing meringues cannot be overemphasized.

Egg whites should be at room temperature — about 75 degrees — and absolutely free of yolk. The bowl and beater should be without the slightest trace of grease. Sugar for meringues may be brown, confectioners', or granulated and should always be free of lumps. Allow about four or five tablespoons of sugar for each egg white.

Meringues should be baked on a clean baking sheet; otherwise they will stick and break during removal. Oven temperature is very important — it should be very slow, about 250 degrees. If the oven is too hot, the meringues will be soft. They are usually removed from the oven and cooled completely before taking them from their baking pan.

In the pages that follow, we've assembled the favorite cheesecake, torte, and meringue recipes from the kitchens of *Southern Living* homemakers. As you browse through them, picture the pleasure your family will get from these light and elegant desserts — and the pleasure you'll get from their warm praises!

BAISERS CREOLES

6 egg whites	1 tsp. vinegar
1/4 tsp. salt	1 tbsp. flour
1 tsp. baking powder	1 tsp. vanilla
2 c. sugar	1/4 tsp. almond extract

Preheat oven to 300 degrees. Combine the egg whites and salt in a bowl and beat until frothy. Sprinkle with baking powder and beat until stiff. Add 3/4 of the sugar, small amount at a time, beating well after each addition. Add vinegar and flour and beat well. Add remaining sugar gradually and beat until thick and glossy. Fold in flavorings. Place in 10 circles on brown paper-lined and greased baking sheets. Bake for 5 minutes. Turn off heat and leave in oven for 1 hour without opening oven door.

Mrs. Pat Ruh, Knoxville, Tennessee

MERINGUE CHANTILLY

8 egg whites	1 tsp. vanilla
1/4 tsp. salt	4 c. sweetened whipped cream
1/4 tsp. cream of tartar	Large fresh strawberries
2 c. sugar	

Grease 2 large baking sheets and line with waxed paper. Draw two 9-inch circles on each sheet of waxed paper. Beat the egg whites in a mixing bowl until frothy. Add the salt and cream of tartar and beat well. Add the sugar, 1 tablespoon at a time, beating constantly. Add vanilla and beat until stiff and glossy. Place 3/4 of the meringue on 3 of the circles. Place remaining meringue in a pastry bag and pipe around rim of remaining circle. Make a lattice by piping 4 strips of meringue horizontally and 4 vertically across circle, touching meringue rim. Bake at 225 degrees for about 45 minutes or until firm and dry, but still white. Cool slightly and remove from waxed paper with a broad spatula. Place 1 solid meringue on a serving dish and spread with 1 cup whipped cream. Top with second solid meringue and add 1 cup whipped cream. Add remaining solid meringue and cover with 1 cup whipped cream. Place lattice meringue on top. Fill pastry bag with remaining whipped cream and pipe decorative swirls on side of layers and a row of rosettes around top. Fill lattice cavities with strawberries. May be refrigerated for about 1 hour before serving. 8 servings.

Mrs. William D. Mallard, Jr., Anniston, Alabama

CHOCOLATE ANGEL MERINGUE

2 egg whites	1/2 c. sugar
1/8 tsp. salt	1/2 c. chopped walnuts or pecans
1/8 tsp. cream of tartar	1/2 tsp. vanilla

Combine the egg whites, salt and cream of tartar in a bowl and beat until foamy. Add sugar, small amount at a time, beating constantly, then beat until stiff. Fold in walnuts and vanilla and spoon into lightly greased 8-inch cake pan, hollowing out center and building sides to 1/2 inch above edge of pan. Bake at 300 degrees for 50 to 55 minutes.

Filling

1 1/4-lb. package sweet cooking chocolate 3 tbsp. water	1 tsp. vanilla 1 c. heavy cream, whipped

Place chocolate and water in a saucepan over low heat and stir until melted. Cool and add vanilla. Fold into whipped cream and fill meringue shell. Chill for 2 hours.

Mrs J. C. Howard, McCarley, Mississippi

CHOCOLATE-ALMOND DELIGHT

4 egg whites, at room temperature 1/4 tsp. cream of tartar 1 c. sugar 1 tsp. instant coffee 1/2 tsp. vanilla	2 qt. Dutch chocolate ice cream 1 c. heavy cream, whipped Chocolate syrup Shelled blanched whole almonds

Beat the egg whites in a bowl until frothy. Sprinkle with cream of tartar and beat until stiff, but not dry. Beat in sugar, 1 tablespoon at a time, adding the instant coffee with the last tablespoon of sugar, and beat until very stiff. Fold in vanilla. Outline a circle on unglazed paper with a 10-inch pie plate and place paper on a baking sheet. Spread meringue about 1 inch deep over the circle and spoon remaining meringue around edge of circle to build up edge. Bake in 275-degree oven for about 1 hour or until light brown and dry. Cool away from drafts. Fill shell with ice cream and circle ice cream with whipped cream. Garnish with chocolate syrup and almonds. Serve immediately. 12 servings.

FRESH PEACH MERINGUE

6 lge. egg whites
1/4 tsp. salt
1/2 tsp. cream of tartar
1 3/4 c. sugar
1 1/2 tsp. vanilla

6 med. fresh peaches
2 tbsp. lemon juice
1 env. unflavored gelatin
2 tbsp. cold water
Vanilla Whipped Cream

Preheat oven to 400 degrees. Place the egg whites, salt and cream of tartar in large mixer bowl and beat with electric mixer until egg whites have doubled in volume. Beat in 1 1/2 cups sugar, 1 tablespoon at a time, being sure each addition of sugar is dissolved before adding the next. Beat in vanilla and spoon into a buttered 8-inch springform pan. Make a depression in center about 5 inches wide and 1 inch deep with the back of a tablespoon. Place in oven, close door and turn off heat. Leave meringue in oven for 12 hours or overnight without opening oven door. Remove from oven and run a spatula around sides to loosen from pan. Release the spring and gently lift off sides of pan. Slide meringue off pan onto a serving plate carefully. Peel and slice peaches and place in a bowl. Sprinkle with lemon juice and remaining sugar. Soften gelatin in cold water and dissolve over hot water. Blend with peach mixture and chill until thickened. Pile into meringue and top with Vanilla Whipped Cream. Garnish with slices of peaches and mint leaves and serve at once.

Vanilla Whipped Cream

1/2 c. heavy cream
1 tbsp. sugar

1/4 tsp. vanilla

Whip the cream in a bowl until stiff and fold in sugar and vanilla.

PEACH SURPRISE

2 egg whites
1/4 c. sugar

Peach halves
Ice cream

Beat the egg whites in a mixing bowl until soft peaks form. Add the sugar gradually and beat until stiff. Fill each peach half with meringue and place on a cookie sheet. Bake at 450 degrees until brown. Place the ice cream in a bowl and place peach meringues on ice cream. Serve immediately.

Mrs. Kathleen E. Houston, Houston, Texas

COFFEE MERINGUES GLACE

2 egg whites	2/3 c. sugar
1/2 tsp. lemon juice	

Combine the egg whites and lemon juice in a bowl and beat until soft peaks form. Add sugar, small amount at a time, beating well after each addition. Beat until stiff and glossy. Shape into 6 circles on lightly greased baking sheet, building up edges to 1/2 inch with back of spoon. Bake at 275 degrees for 25 minutes. Turn off heat and leave in oven until cold.

Bittersweet Chocolate Sauce

1 12-oz. package semisweet chocolate pieces	1 lge. can evaporated milk
	1 qt. coffee ice cream

Melt the chocolate in evaporated milk in a saucepan over low heat, stirring constantly, then cool. Chill. Mound ice cream in meringue shells and pour sauce over ice cream. Serve immediately. 6 servings.

Mrs. Curtis Herbert, Houston, Texas

LEMON ANGEL WHISPER

4 egg whites	1 c. sugar
1/4 tsp. cream of tartar	

Beat the egg whites in a bowl until frothy and add cream of tartar. Add sugar gradually and beat until stiff but not dry. Pour into well-greased 9-inch cake pan. Bake at 250 degrees for 50 minutes to 1 hour and cool on a wire rack.

Filling

3 tbsp. cornstarch	Juice of 1 lemon
1 c. sugar	Grated rind of 1 lemon
1 1/2 c. boiling water	1 tbsp. butter
3 egg yolks, well beaten	

Mix the cornstarch and sugar in a saucepan. Add the boiling water and mix well. Bring to a boil and cook for 2 minutes. Mix the egg yolks, lemon juice, lemon rind and butter and stir into the cornstarch mixture. Remove from heat and cool. Pour into meringue shell. Top with whipped cream, if desired.

Mrs. Audrey Pardue, Park City, Kentucky

MERINGUES NEIGE

4 c. milk	3/4 tsp. vanilla
6 eggs, separated	1 1/2 tbsp. flour
1 1/4 c. sugar	2 pt. fresh strawberries
Salt	1 sq. unsweetened chocolate
1 1/2 c. heavy cream	

Scald the milk in a large skillet. Beat the egg whites in a bowl until frothy. Add 3/4 cup sugar and 1/4 teaspoon salt gradually, beating constantly, then beat until stiff. Drop 3 large mounds of meringue, 1 inch apart, onto scalded milk and cook for 5 minutes, turning once with a slotted spoon. Drain on paper towels. Repeat until all meringue is used and refrigerate until chilled. Scald the heavy cream with vanilla and 1 1/2 cups milk used for meringues in top of a double boiler. Beat the egg yolks until light and beat in remaining sugar, pinch of salt and flour. Stir in small amount of cream mixture and stir back into cream mixture. Cook over hot water, stirring constantly, until mixture coats a spoon. Cool and refrigerate until chilled. Hull, wash and slice strawberries and place in a deep serving dish. Heap meringues over strawberries and pour custard over meringues. Shave chocolate and sprinkle over custard. 8 servings.

Mrs. R. Bonner, Wetumpka, Alabama

CHARM MERINGUE

6 egg whites	Whipped cream
2 c. sugar	Strawberries
2 tsp. baking powder	

Beat the egg whites in a bowl until stiff, adding sugar and baking powder gradually. Place in a greased 9-inch square baking pan. Bake in 250-degree oven for 1 hour and cool. Remove from pan. Cut off top and fill with whipped cream and strawberries. Replace top and spread with whipped cream. Garnish with strawberries.

Mrs. Colon Neeley, Shelbyville, Tennessee

ALMOND HERSHEY TORTE

1 box vanilla wafers	1/2 c. milk
1 lge. chocolate-almond candy bar	1 pt. heavy cream
16 marshmallows	1/2 c. toasted almonds (opt.)

Crush the vanilla wafers into fine crumbs. Sprinkle half the crumbs in 8 1/2 x 11-inch baking pan. Melt the chocolate bar and marshmallows in milk in a double boiler, then cool. Whip the cream until stiff and fold in chocolate mixture. Spread over crumbs and sprinkle remaining crumbs over chocolate mixture. Sprinkle almonds on top. Refrigerate for at least 1 hour before serving. 12 servings.

Mrs. S. Thomas, Montgomery, Alabama

DREAM TORTE

2 pkg. ladyfingers	12 frozen chocolate-toffee candy
2 pkg. dessert topping mix	bars

Line a square baking pan with 1/3 of the ladyfingers. Prepare dessert topping mix according to package directions and spread half the dessert topping over ladyfingers. Crush the candy bars and sprinkle half the candy crumbs over dessert topping. Add half the remaining ladyfingers, then add remaining dessert topping. Add remaining candy crumbs and top with remaining ladyfingers. Refrigerate until chilled.

Mrs. Lloyd Bethune, Port Charlotte, Florida

BANANA-RUM TORTE

3 lge. bananas	1/2 tsp. instant coffee
1 tbsp. lime juice	2 baked 9-in. rum cake layers,
3 tbsp. dark rum	cooled
1 1/2 c. whipping cream	8 Pepperidge Farm Pirouettes
3 tbsp. sugar	

Peel the bananas and slice about 1/4 inch thick. Combine the lime juice and 1 tablespoon rum and pour over banana slices. Beat the whipping cream with sugar and coffee until soft peaks form. Beat in the remaining rum and beat until stiff peaks form. Place cake layers together with half the cream and half the drained banana slices. Top with remaining cream and refrigerate for 30 minutes to 1 hour to mellow. Drain remaining banana slices and arrange on top. Place Pirouettes spoke-fashion on cream. One and 1/2 teaspoons rum extract may be substituted for rum.

SOUR CREAM TORTE

3 c. sifted all-purpose flour	2 c. chopped walnuts or pecans
3/4 c. sugar	2 c. sour cream
1 c. butter or margarine	1 1/2 c. confectioners' sugar
1 egg, beaten	1 tsp. vanilla

Preheat oven to 350 degrees. Mix the flour and sugar in a mixing bowl and cut in the butter until mixture resembles coarse meal. Stir in the egg and mix well. Divide into 7 equal parts and roll each part on lightly floured surface into 9-inch circle. Place on cookie sheet. Bake for 10 to 12 minutes or until the edges are light brown. Cool and remove from cookie sheet with spatula. Mix walnuts with sour cream, confectioners' sugar and vanilla and spread on each baked circle. Place circles on top of each other and sprinkle top with additional confectioners' sugar. Refrigerate for 5 hours or overnight and cut in wedges to serve.

Mrs. Dennis P. Landry, Crowley, Louisiana

GLAMOUR TORTE CAKE

1 pkg. cake mix	1 med. can crushed pineapple
1/2 c. sugar	3/4 c. halved candied cherries
1 tbsp. flour	1/2 pt. whipping cream
1/4 tsp. salt	1 tbsp. confectioners' sugar
2 egg yolks	1/2 tsp. vanilla
1 c. shredded coconut	

Prepare and bake the cake mix in 3 layers according to package directions. Mix the sugar, flour, salt and egg yolks in a saucepan. Stir in coconut and pineapple and cook until thick. Cool. Add the cherries and mix well. Spread on cake layers and place layers together. Beat the whipping cream until stiff and fold in confectioners' sugar and vanilla. Spread on top and side of torte. 12 servings.

Mrs. William O. Whitt, Birmingham, Alabama

CRANBERRY TORTE

3 eggs, separated	1 1-lb. can whole cranberry sauce
1 c. sugar	
1 c. graham cracker crumbs	1/2 c. (packed) brown sugar
1 tsp. vanilla	1 3-oz. package orange gelatin
1 tsp. almond extract	1 pkg. dessert topping mix
1/2 c. chopped nuts	

Beat the egg yolks in a mixing bowl until thick and lemon colored, adding 1/2 cup sugar gradually. Mix in crumbs, vanilla and almond extract. Beat egg whites until frothy, then beat until stiff, adding remaining sugar gradually. Fold into egg yolk mixture and fold in nuts. Spread in 2 greased 8-inch cake pans. Bake at 350 degrees for 25 to 30 minutes, then cool. Mix the cranberry sauce and brown sugar in a saucepan and bring to a boil over moderate heat, stirring constantly.

Remove from heat. Add the gelatin and stir until dissolved. Chill until partially set. Prepare the dessert topping mix according to package directions. Place 1 cake layer on a serving plate and spread half the gelatin mixture on cake. Spread half the dessert topping on gelatin mixture. Place remaining cake layer on dessert topping and cover with remaining gelatin mixture. Spread remaining dessert topping on gelatin mixture and chill until served.

Mrs. Byron M. Graves, Memphis, Tennessee

GRAHAM TORTE

1 2/3 c. graham cracker crumbs	1/4 c. sugar
1 c. chopped walnuts	4 eggs, separated
1 tsp. cinnamon	1/2 c. milk
1/2 tsp. salt	1 1/2 c. canned applesauce
1/2 tsp. ginger	1 pt. heavy cream
1/4 tsp. allspice	3 tbsp. confectioners' sugar
1/2 tsp. baking powder	Shaved sweet chocolate
1/2 c. butter or margarine	Maraschino cherries

Combine first 7 ingredients. Cream the butter in a bowl. Add the sugar gradually and beat until light and fluffy. Add the egg yolks and mix thoroughly. Add the crumb mixture alternately with the milk. Beat egg whites until stiff but not dry and fold into sugar mixture. Pour into 2 waxed paper-lined and greased 8-inch cake pans. Bake in 325-degree oven for 30 to 35 minutes. Cool, then remove from pans. Cool on wire racks. Place the applesauce in a bowl. Whip the cream until stiff and fold in confectioners' sugar. Fold 2/3 of the whipped cream into applesauce and spread between cake layers. Place remaining whipped cream in a pastry tube and pipe around edge and in center of cake. Garnish with chocolate and cherries.

ANGEL TORTE

1 pkg. angel food cake mix	4 egg yolks, beaten slightly
1 c. water	3/4 c. butter
1 1/3 c. instant nonfat dry milk	1/2 tsp. almond flavoring
1 1/2 c. sugar	1 tsp. vanilla
2 tsp. instant coffee	1 1/2 c. toasted slivered almonds

Prepare and bake angel food cake according to package directions. Combine the water, dry milk, sugar, coffee, egg yolks and butter in a heavy saucepan. Cook over medium heat, stirring constantly, until thickened, then cook for 12 minutes longer. Remove from heat. Add flavorings and beat until thick enough to spread. Cut angel food cake into 4 layers and spread each layer with frosting. Sprinkle each layer with almonds and place layers together. One teaspoon rum flavoring and 1/2 cup walnuts may be substituted for almond flavoring and almonds.

Photograph for this recipe on page 40.

ANN SERANNE'S MOCHA TORTE

8 eggs	8 oz. semisweet chocolate
1 c. sugar	1/2 c. strong coffee
1 c. flour	

Beat eggs with sugar in a bowl until thick and lemon colored. Fold in flour. Melt chocolate in coffee over hot water and cool slightly. Fold into flour mixture. Pour into 2 greased and waxed paper-lined 9-inch layer pans. Bake at 350 degrees for 35 minutes or until a toothpick inserted in center comes out clean. Remove from pans and cool on a rack.

Mocha Butter Cream

1 c. sugar	5 oz. semisweet chocolate
1/3 c. water	1/4 c. strong coffee
1/4 tsp. cream of tartar	1 1/2 c. butter
4 egg yolks, beaten	2 tbsp. dark rum

Combine the sugar, water and cream of tartar in a small pan. Bring to a boil, stirring only until sugar dissolves, and cook over high heat until syrup spins a long thread or 236 degrees on a candy thermometer. Beat into egg yolks gradually, then beat until thick. Melt chocolate in coffee over hot water and stir into egg mixture. Beat in butter, small amount at a time, then stir in rum. Chill until thickened and spread most of the mixture between layers and over side and top of torte. Decorate top with remaining Mocha Butter Cream piped through a star tube.

Chocolate Disks

8 oz. semisweet chocolate

Melt the chocolate over hot water. Spread a thin layer evenly over 24 rounds of waxed paper 2 1/2 inches in diameter. Place on a cookie sheet and chill until firm. Remove paper carefully and decorate sides of torte with disks.

Mrs. Earl G. Wheeler, Washington, District of Columbia

MARVELOUS BLUEBERRY CHEESECAKE

1 1/2 c. graham cracker crumbs
2 1/2 c. sugar
1/2 c. melted margarine
2 8-oz. packages cream cheese
4 eggs, slightly beaten

2 tsp. vanilla
1 can blueberry pie filling
1/2 tsp. grated lemon rind
2 tbsp. lemon juice

Combine the graham cracker crumbs, 1/2 cup sugar and margarine and blend well. Press firmly into 13 x 9 x 2-inch pan. Beat the cream cheese in a bowl until smooth. Add the eggs, vanilla and remaining sugar and beat until fluffy. Spread over crumb mixture. Bake in 375-degree oven for about 20 minutes. Remove from oven and cool. Combine the pie filling, lemon rind and lemon juice in a pan and place over low heat. Bring to a boil, stirring constantly and cool. Spread over cream cheese mixture and chill. 12-16 servings.

Mrs. Joe Costello, Prattville, Alabama

CHERRY SUPREME

11 oz. cream cheese
2 c. graham cracker crumbs
1 stick butter, melted
3 tbsp. confectioners' sugar
1 tsp. unflavored gelatin

2 pkg. dessert topping mix
1 c. cold milk
2 tsp. vanilla
1 c. sugar
1 can cherry pie filling

Soften the cream cheese at room temperature. Mix the graham cracker crumbs, butter and confectioners' sugar and press into 8 x 10-inch dish. Prepare gelatin according to package directions and spread over crumb mixture. Chill. Combine dessert topping mix and milk in a bowl and beat with electric mixer until stiff. Add the vanilla, sugar and cream cheese and beat until smooth. Spread over gelatin and top with cherry pie filling. Chill for 1 hour or longer before serving.

Mrs. Ruth S. Conner, Shawsville, Virginia

CHERRY TOPPER

20 graham crackers, crushed
1 stick margarine, melted
1 1/4 c. confectioners' sugar
1 8-oz. package cream cheese
1 tsp. vanilla

1 sm. can crushed pineapple,
   drained
1/2 c. miniature marshmallows
1 pkg. dessert topping mix
1 can cherry pie filling

Mix the cracker crumbs, margarine and 1/4 cup confectioners' sugar and press into 13 x 9 x 1 1/2-inch baking dish. Place the cream cheese, remaining confectioners' sugar, vanilla, pineapple and marshmallows in a bowl and mix well. Prepare the dessert topping mix according to package directions and mix with cream cheese mixture. Spread on crumb mixture and spoon cherry pie filling over top. Refrigerate overnight. 15-18 servings.

Mrs. Richard Fulper, Jr., Oxon Hill, Maryland

PINEAPPLE CHEESECAKE

1 8-oz. package cream cheese
1 c. sugar
1 sm. box lemon gelatin
1 c. hot water
32 graham crackers, crushed

1/4 c. melted butter or margarine
1 lge. can evaporated milk, chilled
1 c. crushed pineapple

Soften the cream cheese at room temperature. Beat cream cheese with sugar in a bowl until smooth. Dissolve the gelatin in hot water and chill until thickened. Reserve 2/3 cup cracker crumbs. Mix remaining crumbs with butter and press into an 8 x 10-inch dish. Whip the milk until stiff, then fold in gelatin, sugar mixture and pineapple. Pour into crumb mixture and sprinkle reserved crumbs on top. Refrigerate for 2 hours.

Mrs. John P. Farmer, Hurt, Virginia

FRUITED CHEESECAKE

Pastry for 2-crust pie
1/2 lb. cottage cheese, well drained
1/2 lb. cream cheese
1/4 c. flour
1/2 tsp. salt
1/2 tsp. vanilla

1/2 tsp. grated lemon rind
2 eggs
1/4 c. melted butter
1 c. hot milk
4 egg whites
3/4 c. sugar
3/4 c. drained crushed pineapple

Roll out the pastry on a floured surface and line the bottom and side of a greased 10-inch springform pan. Bake at 300 degrees for about 15 minutes or until golden brown. Combine the cottage cheese, cream cheese, flour, salt, vanilla, grated rind and eggs in a mixing bowl and mix well with electric mixer. Add the butter and mix. Add the milk and blend thoroughly. Beat the egg whites until stiff, adding sugar gradually, and fold into the cheese mixture. Spread the pineapple over the baked crust and cover with cheese mixture. Bake for 45 minutes longer, then cool. Chill before serving.

Mrs. Charles Freeman, Huntsville, Alabama

STRAWBERRY PLEASURE

2 c. vanilla wafer crumbs
1 stick margarine, melted
1 8-oz. package cream cheese
1 can sweetened condensed milk
1/3 c. lemon juice

1 3-oz. package strawberry gelatin
1 c. boiling water
1 10-oz. package frozen strawberries

Place the wafer crumbs in an oblong dish and pour the butter over crumbs. Mix well and press into dishes. Beat the cream cheese in a bowl until soft and stir in the milk until blended. Mix in lemon juice and spread over crumb mixture. Dissolve the gelatin in boiling water, stir in the strawberries and pour over cream cheese mixture. Chill until firm. Serve topped with whipped cream, if desired.

Mrs. E. F. Males, Antlers, Oklahoma

GLAZED CHEESECAKE PUFFS

1 lb. cream cheese	**1 tsp. vanilla**
3/4 c. sugar	**Vanilla wafers**
2 eggs	**1 can cherry pie filling**

Place the cream cheese, sugar, eggs and vanilla in a large bowl and beat with electric mixer until smooth. Line muffin tins with paper liners and place 1 vanilla wafer in bottom of each liner. Fill liners 3/4 full with cream cheese mixture. Bake at 375 degrees for 10 minutes and cool. Cover with pie filling and chill. 2 dozen.

Mrs. R. C. Scott, Goldsboro, North Carolina

CHEDDAR CHEESECAKE

1 1/4 c. vanilla wafer crumbs	**1/2 tsp. grated orange peel**
2 tbsp. melted butter or margarine	**1/4 tsp. grated lemon peel**
2 8-oz. packages cream cheese	**2 tbsp. flour**
1/2 c. shredded sharp Cheddar cheese	**1 c. heavy cream**
3/4 c. sugar	**1 pt. fresh whole strawberries**
3 eggs	**Light corn syrup**

Mix the crumbs with butter and press over bottom of 9-inch springform pan. Bake in 350-degree oven for 5 minutes. Soften the cream cheese in a bowl, then stir in Cheddar cheese. Add the sugar gradually and beat until fluffy. Beat in the eggs, one at a time. Blend in peels, flour and 1/2 cup cream and pour over crumb crust in pan. Bake for 40 minutes longer or until cake tests done. Cool on a rack. Place the strawberries on top of the cake and brush with corn syrup. Whip remaining cream until stiff. Place in a pastry tube and pipe in a border around the strawberries. 8 servings.

pies

"Wow . . . pie for dessert!"

That one phrase sums up how well-loved pies are. In fact, pies are the all-time favorite American dessert. Southern homemakers understand their families' eagerness for pies and use their cooking skills to satisfy that craving. They also make good use of southern produce.

In mid-summer when peaches hang heavy in the orchards, thousands of southern kitchens are filled with the appetite-appealing smell of fresh-baked peach pies. And on crisp autumn evenings, the aroma of fresh pecan pie is a welcome greeting all over the Southland.

Peach and pecan are just two favorite southern pies. There are many more . . . and in this section you will find the recipes for them all. Tart and tasty lemon meringue pie . . . all-American apple pie . . . rich cream pie . . . recipes for these pies and more are awaiting your reading and cooking pleasure.

Every recipe in this section had its beginning in the creative imagination of a southern homemaker. It was prepared to perfection in her kitchen and won warm words of approval from family and friends. Many recipes even won prizes at state and local fairs. Now these home-tested favorite recipes are gathered here for you to enjoy. Why not bake a pie tonight and hear your family say, "Wow . . . pie for dessert!"

The hallmark of a good pie maker is a flaky crust — ask any blue ribbon winner! The art of making light, flaky crusts is easy to master. Be sure to chill your ingredients — the shortening, the water, even the flour. Chill the utensils, too.

By chilling your ingredients before you begin to prepare your crust, you avoid the possibility of shortening breaking down and blending with flour before the crust is baked. When small particles of chilled shortening melt quickly under great heat and blend with the flour which surrounds them, flakes are produced. The result is layer upon layer of flakes with air spaces between — the sign of truly light pie crust. When shortening breaks down before baking, the result is a hard and brittle pie crust. So rule one is to chill both ingredients and utensils.

cooking methods
FOR PIES

When you are mixing the dough, the proportion of water to flour will vary. Usually, it takes about two to four tablespoons of water to blend one cup of flour and the proportionate amount of shortening. Mix the dough by first blending the amounts of flour and shortening called for in your recipe then adding the water, sprinkling it, a tablespoon at a time, over the flour-shortening mixture. Expert pastry chefs advise that as you sprinkle additional water over your dough, you should try to sprinkle on the remaining dry ingredients rather than onto the already-mixed dough. This hint is a good way to avoid overmixing the dough.

Rule two is to handle the dough lightly and quickly. A pastry blender is a must for good pie crusts — only the very best pastry chefs can handle dough with their fingers so quickly and lightly that their body heat does not warm the shortening to its breakdown point.

After the dough has been properly mixed, chill it in a closed container for at least 12 hours. Chilling will tenderize the dough, help prevent shrinkage, and make it easier to handle. Chilled dough should be removed from the refrigerator at least one hour before it is rolled out.

A stockinette-covered rolling pin and board can minimize the amount of extra flour used in rolling out dough — and help keep your crust light and flaky. If you don't have a covered board, try rolling the dough between two layers of plastic wrap, waxed paper, or aluminum foil. After rolling, you simply peel off one side of paper, fit the dough in the pie pan, and peel off the remaining side.

Roll dough with a light motion from the center outward. Avoid the to-and-fro motion: it may break down shortening particles. If the dough tears, patch it but do not reroll.

What about pie pans? Dull-finish pans will give the most evenly browned pie crust. The exception would be a crumb crust which should be baked in a shiny metal or enamel pan to prevent too much browning. If you use glass or enamelware pans, cut your baking time by one-fifth to one-fourth. And always preheat the oven — preheating helps form the light flakes you want.

How you bake your crust depends in large measure on the kind of pie you are preparing. There are one-crust and two-crust pies. Pie shells for one-crust pies are usually baked and then filled with a cream or custard filling. These shells are baked at very high temperature. To keep the shell from puffing up during baking, try filling it with rice, dried beans, macaroni, or bread crusts. The French use small clean pebbles for the same purpose!

Some single-crust pie recipes may call for the shell to be baked, filled, then returned to the oven — lemon meringue pie is a good example of this. To keep your crust from becoming too brown during this "second baking" try setting the pie plate into another empty pie plate before baking. The extra pan will absorb much of the heat which could make your crust too brown.

Two-crust pies, as the name implies, have a bottom and top crust with a filling between. Most two-crust pies are fruit pies. Roll the bottom dough first, rolling it about 1/8-inch thick. Ease it into the pie plate, avoiding stretching. Press it gently along the bottom and sides of the plate.

Many pie fillings are so juicy that they can make even the flakiest bottom crusts soggy and unappetizing. To overcome this problem, try brushing the bottom crust with an egg white or melted butter before you put in the filling. This hint will also prevent sogginess which may result if your filling is very hot.

Roll the top crust a little thinner than the bottom one. Place over the filling, and trim the overhang of the bottom and top crusts to about 1/2 inch all around. Fold under to seal the pie, and flute the edge.

To prevent this decorative edge from becoming too brown during baking, cover it with a piece of aluminum foil cut about 2 inches wide and 30 inches long. Overlap the ends and seal by folding them over each other.

Make cutouts in your top crust so that steam can escape during baking. Some juices may boil over during baking even with this precaution. But the cutouts will keep this down to a minimum. And to prevent a burned smell and accompanying smoke, sprinkle any juice spills with salt.

Pie-making is not only an achievement — it is fun. Experiment by all means. If your family loves both apple pie and peach pie, try a peach-apple pie filled with both fruits. Strawberry-rhubarb is a favorite combination pie. You'll find many intriguing combinations in this cookbook that will soon have your family and guests praising your pies.

FRENCH APPLE PIE

Pastry for 2-crust pie	**1 tsp. salt**
6 med. tart apples	**2 tbsp. margarine**
1 c. seedless raisins	**1/2 c. confectioners' sugar**
1/2 c. sugar	**2 tsp. water**
1 tsp. cinnamon	

Roll out half the pastry on a floured surface and place in a 9-inch pie pan. Trim edge. Pare, core and slice the apples and mix with raisins. Place in pastry. Mix the sugar, cinnamon and salt and sprinkle over apple mixture. Dot with margarine. Roll out remaining pastry and place over apple mixture. Cut 3 slits in center of pastry and seal edge. Bake at 350 degrees for 40 to 50 minutes or until the apples are tender and crust is browned. Cool. Mix the confectioners' sugar with water and spread over crust.

Mrs. V. C. Hamlin, Ladonia, Texas

APPLE-MACAROON PIE

4 c. thinly sliced apples	**2 tbsp. butter or margarine**
1 unbaked 9-inch pie shell	**1 egg, beaten**
1 c. sugar	**1/4 c. milk**
1 tbsp. flour	**1 c. shredded coconut**
1/2 tsp. salt	

Place the apples in the pie shell. Mix 1/2 cup sugar, flour and salt and sprinkle over apples. Dot with 1 tablespoon butter. Bake at 350 degrees for 20 minutes. Combine remaining sugar and butter, egg, milk and coconut and pour over apple mixture. Bake for 30 minutes longer.

Mrs. C. T. Robertson, Crestwood, Kentucky

APRICOT-CREAM DREAM PIE

1 tbsp. unflavored gelatin	**1 1/2 c. apricot puree**
1/4 c. cold water	**1 c. whipping cream**
2 tbsp. lemon juice	**1 deep 9-in. graham cracker**
1/4 tsp. salt	**crust**
5/8 c. sugar	**1 c. sour cream**

Sprinkle the gelatin over the water in a saucepan and let stand for 5 minutes. Add the lemon juice, salt, 1/2 cup sugar and apricot puree and heat over low heat, stirring constantly, for 8 to 10 minutes or until gelatin is dissolved. Cool, then chill until thickened. Whip the whipping cream with remaining sugar until stiff and fold into apricot mixture. Pour into graham cracker crust and chill for 4 to 6 hours or overnight. Spread sour cream over top of pie and serve.

Mrs. Bertha Block, Charlottesville, Virginia

STRAWBERRY PIE

1 c. sugar	2 c. sliced fresh strawberries
3 tbsp. cornstarch	1 baked 9-in. pie shell
Red food coloring	Whipped cream
1 tsp. lemon juice	

Mix the sugar and 1 cup water in a saucepan and bring to boiling point. Mix the cornstarch with a small amount of water and stir into sugar mixture. Cook until thick and clear, stirring constantly, and remove from heat. Add several drops of food coloring and lemon juice and cool thoroughly. Stir in the strawberries and pour into pie shell. Top with whipped cream and chill for 1 hour before serving.

Mrs. Henry Pratt, Willis, Texas

STRAWBERRY CRUMB PIE

3 pt. fresh strawberries, halved	2 to 3 tbsp. water
3/4 c. sugar	1/4 c. (firmly-packed) light
1/4 c. cornstarch	brown sugar
1 1/3 c. sifted all-purpose flour	1/2 tsp. cinnamon
1/2 tsp. salt	Light cream
1/2 c. shortening	

Combine the strawberries with sugar and cornstarch and set aside. Combine the flour and salt in a bowl and cut in shortening until mixture resembles coarse meal. Reserve 2/3 cup. Sprinkle the water over remaining flour mixture and mix until flour is moistened. Press into a ball. Roll out on lightly floured surface to circle 1 1/2 inches larger than inverted 9-inch pie plate. Fit into plate and trim 1/2 inch beyond edge, then fold under and flute edge. Fill with strawberry mixture. Blend reserved flour mixture, brown sugar and cinnamon and sprinkle over strawberry mixture. Bake in 400-degree oven for 45 minutes or until crust is browned. Serve warm or cool with the cream.

MISS MUFFETT'S PIE

1 c. sifted flour	1/2 c. margarine, softened
1/4 c. sugar	1 egg yolk
1 tsp. grated lemon rind	1/4 tsp. vanilla

Preheat oven to 400 degrees. Mix first 3 ingredients in a bowl and make a well in center. Add remaining ingredients and mix well. Press into bottom and side of 10-inch pie plate and prick with a fork. Bake for 7 minutes, then cool.

Filling

2 12-oz. cartons cottage cheese	1 tsp. grated lemon rind
	5 eggs
1 c. sugar	1 egg white
1 1/2 tbsp. flour	1/4 tsp. vanilla
1/4 tsp. salt	1 tsp. lemon juice

Drain the cottage cheese and place in a mixing bowl. Beat with electric mixer until creamy. Add the sugar, flour, salt and grated rind and mix well. Add eggs and egg white, on at a time, and beat well. Stir in vanilla and lemon juice and pour into pie crust. Bake at 450 degrees for 12 to 15 minutes or until golden. Reduce temperature to 400 degrees and bake for 15 minutes longer or until set.

Topping

1 10-oz. package frozen strawberries	1 tbsp. sugar
	1 1/2 tsp. grated lemon rind
1 1/2 tsp. cornstarch	1 tbsp. lemon juice

Thaw the strawberries and drain, reserving 2 tablespoons juice. Mix the strawberries, reserved juice and remaining ingredients in a saucepan and cook, stirring, until thick and clear. Cool slightly and spoon over pie.

Mrs. Charles B. Elkins, Baton Rouge, Louisiana

CHERRY-NUT PIE

1 can sour red pitted cherries	1/2 pt. cream, whipped
1 can sweetened condensed milk	Juice of 2 lemons
1 c. chopped pecans	2 graham cracker crusts

Drain the cherries and cut in small pieces. Place in a bowl, add the milk and pecans and mix well. Fold in whipped cream and lemon juice. Pour into pie crusts and chill.

Mrs. J. Mitchell Murry, Ft. Campbell, Kentucky

BLACKBERRY PIE

Pastry for 2-crust pie	1/4 tsp. salt
1 pt. blackberries	1/4 c. water
Flour	4 tbsp. butter
1 c. sugar	

Roll out half the pastry on a floured surface and place in a pie plate. Trim edge. Dredge the blackberries with flour and place in pastry. Sprinkle sugar and salt over the blackberries. Add water and dot with butter. Roll out remaining pastry and place over blackberry mixture. Seal edge. Bake at 375 degrees until crust is brown.

Mrs. Charles E. Barnes, Marion, Alabama

CREME DE MENTHE PIE

1 1/4 c. chocolate wafer crumbs	1/2 c. cold water
3/4 c. sugar	1/4 c. green creme de menthe
1/3 c. melted butter or margarine	1/4 c. white creme de cacao
1 env. unflavored gelatin	1 1/2 c. heavy cream
1/8 tsp. salt	Chopped pistachio nuts
3 eggs, separated	Chopped cherries

Mix the wafer crumbs, 1/4 cup sugar and butter and press into 9-inch pie plate. Bake in a 400-degree oven for 5 minutes, then cool. Combine the gelatin, 1/4 cup sugar and salt in a medium saucepan. Beat the egg yolks and water together and stir into gelatin mixture. Cook over low heat, stirring constantly, for 3 to 5 minutes or until thickened and gelatin is dissolved. Remove from heat and stir in the creme de menthe and creme de cacao. Chill, stirring occasionally, until mixture is consistency of unbeaten egg white. Beat the egg whites until stiff but not dry. Add remaining sugar gradually and beat until very stiff. Fold into gelatin mixture. Whip 1 cup cream until stiff and fold into gelatin mixture. Pour into chocolate crust and chill until firm. Whip remaining cream until stiff and place on pie in shape of wreath. Sprinkle with pistachio nuts and cherries.

CHOCOLATE CHESS PIE

1 c. sugar	1/2 c. melted butter or margarine
3 tbsp. cornmeal	1/2 c. light corn syrup
3 tbsp. cocoa	1 tsp. vanilla
3 eggs, well beaten	1 unbaked 9-in. pie crust

Mix the sugar, cornmeal and cocoa in a bowl. Add the eggs, butter, corn syrup and vanilla and mix well. Pour into pie crust. Bake at 350 degrees for 45 minutes.

Mrs. W. E. Stone, Baxley, Georgia

SOUTHERN SWEET CHOCOLATE PIE

1 4-oz. package sweet cooking chocolate	1/8 tsp. salt
	2 eggs
1/4 c. butter	1 tsp. vanilla
1 2/3 c. evaporated milk	1 unbaked 10-in. pie shell
1 1/2 c. sugar	1 1/3 c. flaked coconut
3 tbsp. cornstarch	1/2 c. chopped pecans

Mix the chocolate with butter in a saucepan and place over low heat, stirring constantly, until blended. Remove from heat, then blend in evaporated milk gradually. Mix the sugar, cornstarch and salt in a bowl. Beat in the eggs and vanilla. Blend in chocolate mixture gradually and pour into pie shell. Combine the coconut and pecans and sprinkle over filling. Bake at 375 degrees for 45 to 50 minutes or until puffed and browned. Cover loosely with aluminum foil during the last 15 minutes of baking if topping browns too quickly. Cool for at least 4 hours. Filling will set while cooling. Garnish with dollops of prepared whipped topping, if desired. 10-12 servings.

FRENCH SILK PIE

1 stick butter or margarine	2 eggs
3/4 c. sugar	1 baked pie shell, cooled
1 1/2 sq. unsweetened chocolate	Sweetened whipped cream
1 tsp. vanilla	

Cream the butter and sugar in a bowl. Melt the chocolate over boiling water and stir into creamed mixture. Add vanilla. Add 1 egg and beat with electric mixer for 5 minutes. Add remaining egg and beat for 5 minutes longer. Pour into pie shell and top with whipped cream. Chill.

Mrs. Ralph E. Dial, Concord, Tennessee

GOLDBRICK PIE

1 1/2 sticks butter	4 eggs
1 c. sugar	1/2 c. chopped nuts
3 sq. unsweetened chocolate	1 baked pie shell
1 tsp. vanilla	Whipped cream

Soften the butter at room temperature. Cream the butter and sugar in a bowl. Melt the chocolate over boiling water and cool. Stir into the creamed mixture, then stir in vanilla. Add the eggs, one at a time, beating for 5 minutes after each addition. Add the nuts and pour into pie shell. Top with whipped cream and chill.

Mrs. Douglas W. Darden, Baton Rouge, Louisiana

COCONUT CREAM PIE

6 tbsp. sugar	3 egg yolks, beaten
5 tbsp. flour	1 c. flaked coconut
1/4 tsp. salt	2 tsp. vanilla
2 c. milk	1 baked 9-in. pie shell

Combine the sugar, flour and salt in a saucepan. Add the milk and egg yolks and mix thoroughly. Cook for 10 minutes, stirring constantly. Add coconut and vanilla and cool. Pour into pie shell.

Meringue

3 egg whites	1/2 c. flaked coconut
4 tbsp. sugar	

Beat the egg whites until soft peaks form, then beat until stiff, adding sugar slowly. Spread on pie and sprinkle with coconut. Bake at 425 degrees until brown.

Mrs. R. D. Wilburn, Statham, Georgia

FRENCH COCONUT PIE

3 eggs, beaten	1 tsp. vanilla
1 1/2 c. sugar	1/4 tsp. coconut flavoring
1 c. shredded coconut	1/4 c. soft butter or margarine
1 tbsp. vinegar	1 unbaked pie shell

Combine all ingredients except the pie shell in a bowl and mix well. Pour into pie shell. Bake in 350-degree oven for 30 to 35 minutes.

F. Moore, Norris, Tennessee

COCONUT-APPLE PIE

3/4 c. sugar	1/2 c. flaked coconut
1 tbsp. flour	1/3 c. corn flake crumbs
1 tsp. cinnamon	2 tbsp. melted butter or
1/4 tsp. nutmeg	margarine
5 c. thinly sliced apples	2 tbsp. brown sugar
1 unbaked 9-in. pie crust	

Mix the sugar, flour, cinnamon and nutmeg in a bowl. Add the apples and mix well. Pour into pie crust. Combine the coconut, corn flake crumbs, butter and brown sugar and sprinkle over apple mixture. Bake in 400-degree oven for 45 to 50 minutes or until done.

Susie Nelson, Clinton, Tennessee

BANANA CREAM PIE

1 c. sugar	1 c. water
3 tbsp. cornstarch	1 tsp. vanilla
1/4 tsp. salt	1 baked 9-in. pastry shell
3 eggs, separated	1 1/2 c. sliced ripe bananas
1 c. evaporated milk	

Mix 2/3 cup sugar, cornstarch, salt and egg yolks in a saucepan. Combine the milk and water and stir into the sugar mixture gradually. Cook over low heat, stirring, for about 10 minutes or until thickened. Remove from heat and stir in vanilla. Cover and cool thoroughly. Pour half the custard into pastry shell. Add bananas and cover with remaining custard. Beat the egg whites in a bowl until soft peaks form then beat until stiff, adding remaining sugar gradually. Spread over pie. Bake at 425 degrees until brown. Cool.

Mrs. Plea E. Jones, Oconee, Tennessee

COFFEE PIE

1/2 c. water	1/4 tsp. nutmeg
2 tbsp. instant coffee	1 c. finely chopped nuts
1/2 lb. marshmallows	1 c. whipping cream
2 egg yolks, slightly beaten	1 baked 9-in. graham cracker
1 tsp. vanilla	crust
Dash of salt	

Combine first 3 ingredients in top of a double boiler. Heat over hot water, stirring occasionally, until marshmallows are melted. Stir into egg yolks slowly, then return to double boiler. Cook and stir for 1 to 2 minutes. Stir in vanilla, salt and nutmeg and chill until partially set. Beat until smooth and fold in nuts. Whip the cream until stiff and fold into coffee mixture. Pour into pie shell and chill. Garnish with additional whipped cream, if desired.

Mrs. Henrietta B. Brooks, Hopewell, Virginia

MOCHA LAYERED PIE

1 1/4 c. graham cracker crumbs	1 tsp. vanilla
1/2 c. sugar	1 env. whipped topping mix
1/4 c. soft butter or margarine	1 tbsp. instant quality coffee
1 pkg. chocolate flavor whipped	1 tbsp. cognac (opt.)
dessert mix	Walnut halves (opt.)
1/2 c. cold milk	

Combine the graham cracker crumbs and 1/4 cup sugar in a bowl and mix in the butter. Press on bottom and side of 9-inch pie pan. Bake at 375 degrees for 8 minutes and cool thoroughly. Prepare chocolate dessert mix according to package directions and reserve 1 cup. Pour remaining chocolate mixture into pie crust. Combine the milk, vanilla and whipped topping mix in a chilled deep, narrow bowl and blend thoroughly. Add remaining sugar and instant coffee gradually, beating constantly with electric mixer at high speed, and beat for about 2 minutes or until light and fluffy. Reserve 1 cup. Blend the cognac with remaining coffee mixture and spread over chocolate mixture in pie crust. Blend reserved coffee mixture with reserved chocolate mixture and spread over top of pie. Garnish with walnut halves and chill for 4 hours or longer.

LEMON PIE

6 eggs, separated	Grated rind of 1 lemon
1 1/4 c. sugar	1 tbsp. butter
Juice of 2 lemons	1 baked pie crust

Beat the egg yolks in top of a double boiler until light and stir in 1 cup sugar, lemon juice, grated rind and butter. Cook over hot water until thick, stirring constantly. Beat 3 egg whites in a bowl until stiff, then add egg yolk mixture slowly, beating constantly. Return to double boiler and cook for 2 minutes longer. Pour into crust. Beat remaining egg whites in a bowl until soft peaks form. Beat until stiff, adding remaining sugar gradually, and spread on pie. Bake in 425-degree oven until brown.

Eleanor B. Hyatt, Knoxville, Tennessee

LEMON-SOUR CREAM PIE

1 3/8 c. sugar	1 tsp. grated lemon peel
3 tbsp. cornstarch	1/4 c. lemon juice
Dash of salt	1 c. sour cream
1 c. milk	1 baked 9-in. pastry shell
3 eggs, separated	1/4 tsp. cream of tartar
1/4 c. butter or margarine	

Combine 1 cup sugar, cornstarch and salt in a saucepan and stir in milk slowly. Cook and stir until thickened. Blend small amount of hot mixture into slightly beaten egg yolks, then stir back into hot mixture. Cook and stir for 2 minutes. Add butter, lemon peel and lemon juice. Cover and cool. Fold in sour cream and pour into pastry shell. Beat egg whites with cream of tartar until soft peaks form. Beat until stiff peaks form, adding remaining sugar gradually, and spread on pie. Bake at 350 degrees until brown.

Mrs. James Hodges, East Brewton, Alabama

KEY LIME PIE

1 tbsp. unflavored gelatin	1/4 c. water
1 c. sugar	1 tsp. grated lime peel
1/4 tsp. salt	Green food coloring
4 eggs, separated	1 c. heavy cream, whipped
1/2 c. lime juice	1 baked 9-in. pie shell

Mix the gelatin, 1/2 cup sugar and salt in a saucepan. Beat egg yolks, lime juice and water together and stir into gelatin mixture. Cook over medium heat, stirring constantly, until mixture comes to a boil. Remove from heat and stir in grated peel. Add enough food coloring for a pale green color. Chill, stirring occasionally, until thickened. Beat egg whites until soft peaks form. Add remaining sugar gradually and beat until stiff peaks form. Fold gelatin mixture into egg whites and fold in whipped cream. Spoon into pastry shell and chill until firm. Spread with additional whipped cream and sprinkle additional grated lime peel around edge of pie.

Mrs. Mary Erb, Ft. Lauderdale, Florida

MOLASSES-PECAN PIE

3 eggs, slightly beaten
3/4 c. unsulphured molasses
3/4 c. light corn syrup
2 tbsp. melted butter or margarine
1/8 tsp. salt

1 tsp. vanilla
1 tbsp. flour
1 c. pecans
1 unbaked 8-in. pastry shell

Combine the eggs, molasses, corn syrup, butter, salt and vanilla in a mixing bowl and mix well. Mix the flour with small amount of egg mixture and stir into remaining egg mixture. Add the pecans and turn into pastry shell. Bake at 325 degrees for 1 hour or until firm.

NEW ORLEANS PECAN PIE

3 eggs, separated
1 c. sour cream
1 c. sugar
4 tbsp. cornstarch
1/4 tsp. grated lemon rind

Pinch of salt
1 baked pie shell, cooled
1 c. (packed) brown sugar
1 c. chopped pecans

Mix the egg yolks, sour cream, sugar, cornstarch, lemon rind and salt in top of a double boiler and cook over boiling water until thick, stirring constantly. Pour into pie shell. Beat the egg whites until stiff, adding brown sugar slowly. Fold in pecans and spread over filling. Bake at 425 degrees until lightly browned. Refrigerate for several hours before serving. One-fourth teaspoon lemon extract may be substituted for grated lemon rind.

Mrs. Edna Clotfelter, Birmingham, Alabama

PEANUT PIE

1 c. dark corn syrup	1/4 tsp. salt
3 eggs	1 c. whole parched peanuts
3 tbsp. flour	1 unbaked 8-in. pastry shell
2 tbsp. melted butter	

Combine the corn syrup, eggs, flour, butter and salt in a mixing bowl and beat with rotary beater for 1 minute. Spread peanuts in pastry shell and pour egg mixture over peanuts. Bake at 350 degrees for 30 minutes.

Mrs. A. B. Alexander, Winston-Salem, North Carolina

GOLD CREST PIE

1 c. sifted flour	1/4 c. sugar
1/2 tsp. salt	1 1/2 tbsp. cornstarch
1/3 c. shortening	1 tsp. grated lemon rind
2 to 3 tbsp. cold water	1/2 c. heavy cream
1 1-lb. can cling peach slices	1 tsp. brown sugar
1 1/2 c. mincemeat	1/2 tsp. pumpkin pie spice

Mix the flour and salt in a bowl and cut in shortening until mixture is consistency of coarse meal. Sprinkle with cold water and mix just until flour is moistened. Shape into a ball and roll out on floured board to an 11-inch circle. Fit into a 9-inch pie plate, turn edge under and crimp. Prick bottom and side of pastry with fork. Bake at 450 degrees for 10 to 12 minutes and cool. Drain syrup from peaches into saucepan and reserve 6 to 8 peach slices for garnish. Chop remaining peach slices and add to the syrup. Add the mincemeat, sugar, cornstarch and lemon rind and mix well. Bring to a boil over medium heat, stirring constantly, and cook until thickened and clear. Turn into pie shell and cool thoroughly. Whip the cream until stiff and fold in brown sugar and spice. Spoon over pie in wide border and garnish with reserved peach slices.

DEEP-DISH PEACH PIE

1 recipe pie pastry
4 peaches, halved
1 1/4 c. sugar

1/2 c. (packed) brown sugar
1 stick butter or margarine
3 eggs, beaten

Line a deep pie plate with pastry and place the peaches, cut side up, in pastry. Sprinkle 1 cup sugar over peaches. Bake at 400 degrees until peaches are tender. Cream remaining sugar, brown sugar and butter in a bowl. Add the eggs and mix well. Pour over peaches and bake until set.

Mrs. J. T. Sowders, Richmond, Kentucky

CREAM CHEESE-PEACH PIE

1 3-oz. package cream cheese
1 baked pastry shell
7 peaches, sliced
1 c. sugar

1/4 c. water
2 tbsp. cornstarch
1 tsp. almond flavoring
Whipped cream

Soften the cream cheese and spread over pastry shell. Place 5 sliced peaches over pastry shell. Combine the sugar, water, cornstarch and remaining peaches in a saucepan and cook, stirring, until thickened. Cool and add almond flavoring. Pour over peaches in the pastry shell and chill. Top with whipped cream and serve.

Mrs. Alton M. Phelps, Jupiter, Florida

PEACH PIE SUPREME

1 recipe pie pastry
5 ripe firm peaches, halved
1 c. sugar

1/3 c. butter or margarine
1/3 c. flour

Line a pie plate with pastry and arrange peach halves in pastry, cut side up. Mix the sugar, butter and flour until mixture resembles coarse cornmeal and sprinkle over peaches. Bake at 400 degrees for 10 minutes. Reduce temperature to 350 degrees and bake for 30 to 40 minutes longer.

Mrs. A. P. Ford, Montgomery, Alabama

PIE CRUST

5 c. flour
1 tsp. salt
1 lb. shortening

1 egg, beaten
1 tbsp. vinegar
Cold water

Place the flour and salt in a bowl. Cut in shortening until mixture resembles cornmeal. Mix the egg and vinegar and add enough water to make 1 cup liquid. Mix with flour mixture. Wrap in waxed paper and place in refrigerator until chilled. Will keep in refrigerator for 1 month.

Emma Gates, Pryor, Oklahoma

PIE CRUST FOR BRIDES

2 c. flour	1 tsp. vinegar
1 tsp. salt	1 egg
3/4 c. shortening	5 or 6 tbsp. water

Sift the flour and salt together into a bowl. Add the shortening and blend until mixture resembles meal. Add vinegar and egg and mix. Add water, 1 tablespoon at a time, until ingredients hold together. Pastry for 2 crusts.

Mrs. J. A. McAnear, Clarendon, Texas

THREE-FRUIT PIE

2 3 1/4-oz. packages lemon pie filling mix	1 1/2 c. pineapple juice
1 1/4 c. sugar	1 2/3 c. graham cracker crumbs
1 1/2 c. orange juice	1/4 c. softened butter or margarine
4 eggs, separated	1/2 c. shredded coconut

Mix the lemon pie filling mix with 1/2 cup sugar and 1/2 cup orange juice in a saucepan. Add the egg yolks and blend well. Add remaining orange juice and pineapple juice. Cook, stirring constantly, over medium heat for 5 to 7 minutes or until thickened, then cool. Mix the graham cracker crumbs, butter and 1/4 cup sugar and press into a 9-inch pie plate. Bake at 375 degrees for 8 minutes, then cool. Pour filling into crust. Beat the egg whites until stiff but not dry, adding remaining sugar gradually. Pile over filling and seal to edges of crust. Sprinkle coconut on top. Bake at 500 degrees for 4 to 5 minutes. Chill for 2 to 3 hours. 6-8 servings.

Photograph for this recipe on page 56.

PINEAPPLE ICEBOX PIE

2/3 c. crushed vanilla wafers	2/3 c. chopped pecans
1/2 c. soft butter	1 1-lb. 4 1/2-oz. can crushed pineapple
1 1/2 c. sifted powdered sugar	1 c. heavy cream, whipped
1 egg, beaten	

Spread the wafer crumbs over bottom and side of well-buttered 9-inch pie pan. Cream the butter and sugar in a bowl until fluffy. Add the egg and pecans and mix well. Drain the pineapple and fold into the butter mixture. Fold in whipped cream and spread over wafer crust. Refrigerate for 24 hours.

Mrs. H. G. Davis, Metairie, Louisiana

FRENCH PINEAPPLE PIE

1 c. margarine or butter	1/2 pt. heavy cream
1 c. crushed vanilla wafers	1 c. drained crushed pineapple
2 c. powdered sugar	1 1/2 c. chopped pecans
4 egg yolks	1 sm. bottle maraschino cherries
1 tsp. vanilla	

Cream 1/2 cup margarine and mix with wafer crumbs. Press half the mixture on bottom and side of pie pan. Cream remaining margarine in a bowl and add powdered sugar slowly, beating constantly. Add the egg yolks, one at a time. Add the vanilla and beat until smooth. Spread over wafer crust. Whip the heavy cream until stiff and fold in pineapple and pecans. Chop the cherries and fold into the whipped cream mixture. Spread over egg yolk mixture and top with remaining wafer mixture. Chill for 24 hours.

Mrs. Harry Sanders, Chamblee, Georgia

ORANGE MERINGUE PIE

1 5/8 c. sugar	1 tbsp. grated orange rind
7 tbsp. cornstarch	1/4 tsp. grated lime rind
3/4 tsp. salt	1/2 c. orange juice
1 1/2 c. warm water	2 tbsp. butter
3 eggs, separated	1 baked 9-in. pie shell

Mix 1 1/4 cups sugar, cornstarch and 1/2 teaspoon salt in a heavy saucepan and stir in warm water. Bring to a boil over low heat, stirring constantly, then cook, stirring constantly, for 8 to 10 minutes or until clear and thick. Remove from heat. Stir several spoons of hot mixture into beaten egg yolks and mix well. Pour back into saucepan, stirring, and bring to a boil. Add the grated rinds and cook over low heat for 4 to 5 minutes. Remove from heat and stir in orange juice and butter. Cool and pour into pie shell. Chill. Place egg whites and remaining salt in a medium bowl and beat until soft peaks form. Add remaining sugar, 1 table-spoon at a time, beating well after each addition, and beat until stiff peaks form. Spread over filling, securing meringue to edge of pie shell. Bake in 425-degree oven for 4 minutes or until meringue is golden.

small pastries, tarts, & cookies

The very sight of a chock-full cookie jar brings back happy memories of childhood raids to get just one more cookie. Yes, cookies are favorites with children – and with adults, too! In fact, cookies, small pastries, and tarts are favorites with everyone who enjoys finger-tip sweets.

Small enough to handle easily but large enough to satisfy the heartiest appetite – that's a good way to describe these delicious taste treats. For chocolate-y goodness, nothing beats a brownie . . . unless it's a creamy smooth chocolate filling in a crisp tart crust. At those leisurely late afternoon get-togethers, marvelously shaped cookies, fruit-filled tarts, and elegant napoleons are certain to be a hit with your guests. And if you really want to see faces light up around your dinner table, carry in a platter full of steaming hot fried pies.

Recipes for these individual-sized taste treats have been gathered in the following section from homemakers all across the Southland. These are recipes shared by women who enjoy cooking for the pleasure of their families and guests – women whose cooking skills have been a big part of that legendary southern hospitality. With folks getting so much finger-licking pleasure out of small pastries, tarts, and cookies, these thoughtful homemakers just naturally spent a long time perfecting their favorite recipes. The results – some of the most outstanding recipes you'll ever find. Try them . . . you'll agree!

These easy-to-handle treats are among the most versatile of all desserts. At a buffet party or just for snacks, small pastries, tarts, and most especially, cookies are universal favorites.

Tarts — small pastry shells filled with jelly, custard, or fruit filling — are particularly good as party desserts where the emphasis is upon finger foods. And they're so easy to make. Just prepare your favorite pastry recipe and roll it out. Cut circles to fit muffin tins or tart pans. Ease in the pastry dough, make a decorative edge, prick the shell, and bake according to directions. Presto! You have tart shells ready for your favorite filling.

Small pastries, in contrast to tarts, have their filling between two layers of pastry. A small pastry may be a mouth-watering dumpling — peach, apple, or

cooking methods

FOR SMALL PASTRIES, TARTS, AND COOKIES

whatever suits your fancy. It may be an elegant cream puff or eclair. Or it may be a fritter — also known as a fried pie. And, there are also the rolled small pastries— elegant napoleons and other extra-special dessert treats.

Here's a hint for quick and easy small pastries for those rainy-day tea parties children love. Form your leftover pie crust scraps into a ball and chill. Then roll flat into an oblong shape. Sprinkle the rolled crust with a thick layer of cinnamon and sugar. Roll up tightly — like a jelly roll — and chill again, for at least an hour. With a sharp knife, slice the pastry roll into tiny circles and bake in a hot oven. What could be more perfect! And these pastry wheels are so easy to make, even your children can share the fun.

Cookies are the most versatile of the small dessert treats. Cookies are perfect for mid-morning, afternoon, or late evening snacks. They make delightful desserts in themselves or as accompaniments to puddings, ice creams, or custards. There are five different types of cookies — bar, drop, molded, pressed, or rolled. They each have special characteristics and all are equally delicious!

Bar cookies are baked in a four-sided pan and have a thin, delicate crust. After baking, they are sliced into bars or squares — like brownies, the most popular bar cookie.

Drop cookies are — as their name implies — dropped from a teaspoon onto a baking sheet. They have a slightly molded shape and are delicate brown, crisp, and tender.

Molded and pressed cookies are two variations of shaped cookies. The difference lies in the shaping method: molded cookies are shaped by hand and pressed cookies are shaped by a mechanical cookie press. The dough is pushed through a cookie press which forms a variety of shapes.

Rolled cookies are made from very soft dough. The dough is always chilled before rolling. Chilled dough is rolled, a small portion at a time, and the remaining dough is kept cold. After rolling, the cookies are cut into the desired shapes. Scraps of dough can be rolled into a ball, rechilled, and rerolled. However, the cookies from this recycled dough will not be as tender as the original batch.

CHOOSING YOUR PAN

An important part of successful cookie-baking is choosing the right pan. Except for bar cookies, always use a cookie sheet. If you don't have a cookie sheet, turn over a baking pan and use the bottom. In baking bar cookies, be sure to use the size pan specified. Too small a pan will produce cake-like cookies; too large will give you dry and brittle cookies. If your cookie recipe includes a lot of fat, don't grease the pan. If you do grease your pan, be sure to use a non-salt agent such as butter or vegetable oil.

BAKING COOKIES

Preheat the oven, and use only one rack. If you place your cookie sheets on two or more racks, the bottoms of the cookies in one pan and the tops of the cookies in the other will be too well done. Check your cookies at the end of the minimum baking time. You can test their doneness by gently pressing their tops. They are done to perfection when the tops spring back. After you remove the sheets from the oven, take the cookies off immediately and let them cool on a rack. And never stack warm cookies one on top of the other.

STORING COOKIES

How you store your cookies will depend on their type. Soft cookies are placed in a tightly-covered container. Bars and squares can be left in their baking pan and covered with plastic wrap or aluminum foil. Crisp cookies store best in a container with a loosely-fitting lid.

To keep soft cookies fresh, add an apple slice, orange segment, or a piece of bread to the cookie jar. Be sure to wrap whatever you put in – it should never come in direct contact with the cookies.

If your crisp cookies become limp, put them in a 300-degree oven for 5 minutes. This trick works well with limp store-bought cookies, too.

MAILING COOKIES

When a member of the family is far from home, nothing says "we're thinking of you" quite as well as a package of home-baked cookies. Choose a sturdy aluminum or cardboard container. Line the container with aluminum foil or waxed paper and put a cushion of crushed paper, popcorn, cereal, or marshmallows on the bottom. Put in a layer of cookies, another cushion, another layer of cookies until the box is filled. Wrap carefully and mark the name and address clearly. It also helps to mark the box "Fragile – Handle With Care." Soft cookies and bars travel best; crisp cookies may break.

APPLE DUMPLING DELIGHT

2 1/2 c. sifted flour	1 1/2 c. sugar
3/4 tsp. salt	1 3/4 tsp. cinnamon
3/4 c. shortening	5 tbsp. butter
7 to 8 tbsp. ice water	2 c. water
6 med. tart apples	

Sift the flour and salt together into a mixing bowl. Cut in shortening with a pastry blender until mixture resembles meal. Sprinkle with ice water and blend with a fork until pastry holds together. Roll out 1/8 inch thick on a lightly floured board and cut into six 7-inch squares. Pare and core the apples and place on pastry squares. Mix 1/2 cup sugar and 1 1/2 teaspoons cinnamon and fill apple cavities with sugar mixture. Dot each apple with 1/6 tablespoon butter. Moisten points of pastry squares. Bring opposite points up over apples, overlapping, and seal well. Place 2 inches apart in 8 x 12-inch baking pan and chill. Mix water and remaining sugar, cinnamon and butter in a saucepan and boil for 3 minutes. Pour around dumplings in baking pan. Bake at 500 degrees for 5 minutes. Reduce temperature to 350 degrees and bake for 30 to 35 minutes longer. Serve warm.

Mrs. Dan P. Johnston, Dallas, Texas

CINNAMON-APPLE DUMPLINGS

2 1/2 c. sifted flour	6 med. tart apples
1 1/2 tsp. salt	2 tbsp. raisins
3/4 c. oats	2 tbsp. brown sugar
1 c. shortening	2 tbsp. melted butter
8 to 9 tbsp. water	

Sift flour and salt together into a bowl and add oats. Cut in the shortening until mixture resembles coarse crumbs. Stir in water gradually and divide into 6 parts. Roll out on floured surface to form 8-inch squares. Peel and core the apples and place 1 apple in center of each pastry square. Combine the raisins, brown sugar and butter and fill apple centers. Bring pastry up over apple, pinching edges together and prick surface. Place in a shallow baking pan. Bake at 425 degrees for 40 minutes or until apples are tender.

Sauce

1/2 c. sugar	1/2 tsp. cinnamon
1 tbsp. cornstarch	1 c. hot water
1/4 tsp. salt	Red food coloring
3 tbsp. red cinnamon candies	

Combine the sugar, cornstarch, salt, candies and cinnamon in a saucepan. Add water and several drops of food coloring and bring to a boil, stirring occasionally. Serve over dumplings.

Mrs. Faith Andrews, Clinton, Tennessee

APPLE DUMPLINGS WITH GINGER SAUCE

1 recipe pie pastry	**1 c. sugar**
4 or 5 lge. tart apples	**3 tbsp. butter**
3 tbsp. hot water	

Roll out the pastry on a floured surface into a rectangle and cut into 6 squares. Pare, core and slice the apples and place in center of each pastry square. Wet edges of pastry and bring together to form a triangle. Seal edges with a fork and prick top. Pour the water into a large, greased baking dish and place dumplings in water. Sprinkle with sugar and dot with butter. Bake at 400 degrees for 35 to 45 minutes.

Ginger Sauce

1 c. sugar	**3 tbsp. chopped crystallized**
2 tbsp. flour	**ginger**
2 tbsp. butter	**3/4 c. milk or water**

Combine first 4 ingredients in a saucepan. Add the milk and mix well. Cook until thick, stirring constantly, and serve with dumplings. One teaspoon ground ginger may be substituted for crystallized ginger.

Mrs. B. C. Blake, Laurinburg, North Carolina

RAISIN-APPLE DUMPLING

3 tart apples	**1/2 c. sugar**
1/2 recipe pie pastry	**Cinnamon to taste**
1/2 c. seedless raisins	**1 tbsp. butter**

Peel, core and slice the apples. Roll out the pastry on a floured surface into a rectangle about 1/2 inch thick. Cover with apples and raisins and sprinkle with sugar and cinnamon. Dot with butter. Roll as for jelly roll and place on a cookie sheet. Bake in 450-degree oven for 15 minutes. Reduce temperature to 350 degrees and bake until apples are tender. Slice and serve hot with hard sauce.

Ola Lee Garrett, Tempson, Texas

PEACH DUMPLINGS

1 qt. sliced peaches	**2 tsp. baking powder**
2 c. sugar	**1/2 c. shortening**
Cinnamon to taste	**3/4 c. (about) water**
2 c. flour	**1 stick butter or margarine**
1/2 tsp. salt	

Mix the peaches, sugar and cinnamon and set aside. Sift the flour, salt and baking powder together into a bowl and cut in shortening. Add enough water to make a soft dough. Roll out on floured board to a rectangle and cut into squares. Fill pastry squares with sweetened peaches and dot with butter. Fold pastry over and seal edges. Place in a baking dish. Bake at 400 degrees for about 45 minutes. Serve with whipped cream, if desired.

Mattie L. Hatchen, Drake Branch, Virginia

APPLE CHEESE-OVERS

2 c. canned applesauce	1/2 tsp. baking powder
1 tsp. cinnamon	1/4 tsp. salt
1 tsp. cornstarch	1/2 c. butter
1 tbsp. cold water	1 3-oz. package cream cheese
1 c. (scant) flour	3/4 c. shredded sharp cheese

Mix the applesauce and cinnamon in a saucepan. Mix the cornstarch with cold water and stir into applesauce mixture. Cook, stirring, over moderate heat for about 15 minutes or until mixture is almost dry, then cool. Combine the flour, baking powder and salt in a bowl and cut in butter and cream cheese. Shape into a ball and chill. Roll out on a floured surface and cut into 3-inch rounds. Place 1 tablespoon applesauce mixture and 1 teaspoon shredded cheese on half of each round and moisten edges. Fold over and press edges together. Pierce top several times with a fork to release steam and place on a cookie sheet. Bake at 425 degrees for 15 minutes or until browned. Sprinkle top lightly with sugar, if desired, and serve hot. 3 dozen.

DRIED FRUIT HALF-MOON PIES

1 1-lb. package dried fruit	1 recipe pie pastry
Sugar to taste	Shortening

Cook the dried fruit according to package directions until tender and add sugar. Roll out pastry into circles and place fruit on half the circles. Fold over and seal edges of pastry with fork. Fry in small amount of hot shortening until browned on both sides.

Wilma Rives, Bear Creek, North Carolina

FRIED CHOCOLATE PIES

1 1/2 c. sugar	**1 tsp. vanilla**
1/2 c. cocoa	**Pastry dough**
Evaporated milk	

Sift the sugar and cocoa together into a bowl and stir in just enough milk to moisten. Add vanilla and mix well. Roll out pastry into circles size of a saucer and place 1 tablespoon filling on 1 side of circles. Fold pastry over and seal edges. Prick tops with a fork. Fry in deep fat until golden brown and drain on paper towels.

Mrs. T. E. Brower, Rogers, Arkansas

GOLDEN-FRIED PEACH PIES

1 1/2 c. self-rising flour	**1 can peaches**
4 tbsp. shortening	**1/2 tbsp. cinnamon**
4 to 5 tbsp. water	**1 tbsp. melted butter**

Sift the flour into a bowl and cut in shortening. Add enough water gradually to hold pastry together and press into a ball. Divide into 5 parts and roll each part on a floured surface into a 5-inch circle. Drain the peaches and mash. Add the cinnamon and butter and mix well. Place 2 tablespoons peach mixture on each circle and fold over. Seal edges with a wet fork. Fry in deep fat at 375 degrees until golden brown and drain on absorbent paper.

Mrs. Warren C. Mitchell, Appalachia, Virginia

ST. JOSEPH'S CREAM PUFFS

1 c. hot water	**1/2 tsp. grated lemon rind**
1/2 c. butter	**1/2 tsp. grated orange rind**
1 c. sifted flour	**24 maraschino cherries, chopped**
4 eggs	

Mix the water and butter in a saucepan and bring to a boil. Add the flour and cook over medium heat, stirring constantly, for 2 minutes or until mixture leaves side of pan. Remove from heat and cool slightly. Add the eggs, one at a time, beating well after each addition. Add grated rinds and cherries and blend. Drop by tablespoonfuls 2 inches apart onto ungreased cookie sheet. Bake at 350 degrees for 30 minutes. Cut an opening in middle of each top and cool thoroughly.

Filling

2 eggs, slightly beaten	**1 c. milk**
3 tbsp. sugar	**1/2 tsp. almond flavoring**
1 tbsp. cornstarch	

Mix all ingredients except almond flavoring in a saucepan. Cook over low heat for 10 minutes or until thick, stirring constantly. Cool slightly and add almond flavoring. Fill puffs and store in refrigerator. 24 cream puffs.

Mrs. Mary C. Antonellis, Hobe Sound, Florida

PISTACHIO PUFFS

8 to 10 baked cooled cream puffs
1 1/2 c. cold milk
1/2 c. heavy cream
1 pkg. instant pistachio
    pudding mix

1/4 c. chopped drained maraschino
    cherries
Confectioners' sugar

Remove tops from the cream puffs and hollow out centers. Reserve tops. Combine the milk and heavy cream in a mixing bowl. Add the pudding mix and beat with an egg beater for about 1 minute or until well blended. Let set for about 5 minutes. Fold in the cherries and let set for 5 minutes longer. Spoon into cream puffs and replace reserved tops. Chill until firm. Sprinkle with confectioners' sugar just before serving.

CREAM PUFFS

1/2 c. butter
1 c. boiling water

1 c. sifted flour
4 eggs

Place the butter and water in a saucepan and bring to boiling point. Add the flour all at once and cook, stirring constantly, until mixture leaves side of saucepan and forms a ball. Remove from heat and cool slightly. Add eggs, one at a time, beating thoroughly after each addition. Drop from tablespoon 3 inches apart on a baking sheet. Bake in a 425-degree oven for 30 to 35 minutes or until golden brown. Remove from oven and cut a slit in side of each. Bake for 2 to 3 minutes longer, then cool on wire rack. Fill with sweetened whipped cream or desired filling. 6-8 cream puffs.

Photograph for this recipe on page 74.

APRICOT STRUDEL

1/4 lb. margarine, softened
1/4 lb. butter, softened

1/2 pt. sour cream
2 1/2 c. flour

Dash of salt
1 1-lb. jar apricot preserves

1 pkg. shredded coconut
1 c. chopped nuts

Mix the margarine and butter in a bowl and add sour cream. Mix the flour and salt. Add to sour cream mixture and mix well. Refrigerate overnight. Divide into 4 parts and roll each part out on a floured pastry cloth to 12 x 15-inch rectangle. Spread each with 1/4 of the apricot preserves and sprinkle with 1/4 of the coconut and nuts. Roll as for jelly roll and place on ungreased cookie sheet. Bake at 350 degrees for 40 to 45 minutes or until golden brown. Slice diagonally while warm. 20 servings.

Mrs. Arnold Shostak, Arlington, Virginia

PALAC SINT

1 recipe biscuit dough
Melted butter

Sugar to taste
Pitted ripe cherries

Roll out the biscuit dough on floured surface into a rectangle 1 inch thick. Brush with melted butter and sprinkle with sugar. Cover with cherries. Roll as for jelly roll and slice. Place on a baking sheet, cut side down. Bake at 350 degrees for about 40 minutes or until done. Serve hot with desired sauce.

Mrs. Edith S. Maness, Robbins, North Carolina

GEORGIA TART

1/2 c. butter
1 c. sugar
2 eggs
1 tsp. vanilla
3 tbsp. milk

1 c. chopped pecans
1 c. raisins
1 c. flaked coconut
1 recipe pie pastry

Cream the butter and sugar in a bowl. Add eggs, vanilla and milk and mix well. Add remaining ingredients except pastry and mix thoroughly. Roll out pastry on a floured surface and cut into 4-inch circles. Place circles in well-greased muffin cups and fill each cup with pecan mixture. Bake at 300 degrees for 30 minutes or until done.

Mrs. W. J. Fowler, Pineview, Georgia

FAVORITE TARTS

1 sm. package cream cheese
2 sticks butter
1 c. flour
Pinch of salt

1 c. sugar
2 eggs, slightly beaten
1 c. seedless raisins
1 c. chopped pecans

Mix the cream cheese and 1 stick butter in a mixing bowl. Add the flour and salt and mix well. Press into muffin tins. Cream remaining butter and sugar in a bowl. Add eggs, raisins and pecans and mix well. Spoon into crust. Bake at 350 degrees for 25 minutes. 16 tarts.

Mrs. Gladys R. Gordner, Greensboro, North Carolina

MINCEMEAT ROLL

1 1/2 c. flour	1/2 c. crushed pineapple
2 tsp. baking powder	2 c. mincemeat
3 tbsp. (rounded) shortening	2 c. (packed) light brown sugar
Milk	2 c. water

Mix the flour and baking powder in a bowl and cut in the shortening. Add enough milk for stiff dough and mix well. Roll out on a floured surface into a rectangle 1/3 inch thick. Mix the pineapple with mincemeat and spread on pastry. Roll as for jelly roll and place in a baking pan. Mix the brown sugar and water in a saucepan and bring to a boil. Pour over and around the roll. Bake in 350-degree oven for 45 minutes. Slice and garnish with maraschino cherries. 8 servings.

Mrs. James H. Lambert, Butler, Kentucky

CHERRY-CHEESE TARTS

1 c. grated cheese	1/8 tsp. salt
1 stick butter, softened	1 c. dark red sweet canned cherries,
2 c. flour	drained

Combine the cheese, butter, flour and salt in a bowl and mix well. Roll out on a floured surface and cut into 2-inch squares. Place 1 tablespoon cherries in center of each square and fold over. Seal edges. Place on a cookie sheet. Bake at 375 degrees until lightly browned.

M. K. Brown, Pegram, Tennessee

DATE-FILLED PASTRIES

1 6-oz. package pitted dates	1/4 lb. grated sharp cheese
1/2 c. (packed) brown sugar	1 1/3 c. sifted flour
1/2 c. butter	1/4 tsp. salt

Chop the dates and place in a saucepan. Add the brown sugar and 1/4 cup water and mix well. Cook over medium heat until thick, then cool. Cream the butter and cheese in a mixing bowl until light. Sift the flour with salt and blend into creamed mixture. Add 2 tablespoons water and mix well. Chill for 1 hour. Roll out 1/8 inch thick on a well-floured surface and cut into 2 3/4-inch circles. Place 1/2 teaspoon date filling on each circle and fold in half. Seal with a fork. Place on ungreased baking sheet. Bake at 375 degrees for 8 to 10 minutes. Cool slightly before removing from baking sheet. 2 dozen.

Mrs. Vernon L. Anderson, Norfolk, Virginia

FRUIT TARTS

1 c. butter	2 eggs
1 3-oz. package cream cheese	1 c. raisins or chopped dates
1 1/2 c. sifted flour	1 c. chopped nuts
1 c. sugar	Confectioners' sugar

Cream 1/2 cup butter and cream cheese in a bowl. Add the flour and mix well. Roll out on floured waxed paper and cut with a biscuit cutter. Place in small greased muffin cups. Cream remaining butter and sugar in a bowl. Add eggs, one at a time, and beat well. Add the raisins and nuts and mix thoroughly. Place in pastry. Bake in 350-degree oven for 15 to 20 minutes and remove from muffin pan while hot. Sprinkle with confectioners' sugar. 2 dozen.

Erma E. Holland, Savannah, Georgia

BLUEBERRY-LIME TARTS

1 12-oz. package frozen blueberries, thawed	1/2 c. lime juice
7/8 c. sugar	2 eggs, separated
1 tbsp. cornstarch	1 tsp. grated lime rind
1/4 tsp. salt	1/3 c. cold water
2 tsp. lemon juice	1/2 c. instant nonfat dry milk
1 tbsp. butter	2 to 3 drops of green food coloring
1/2 env. unflavored gelatin	8 baked tart shells

Drain the blueberries, reserving 1/2 cup syrup. Mix 2 tablespoons sugar, cornstarch and 1/8 teaspoon salt in a 1-quart saucepan and add reserved syrup. Cook, stirring constantly, until thickened and clear, then cook for 3 minutes longer. Stir in the lemon juice and butter and remove from heat. Add the blueberries and chill. Mix the gelatin and remaining sugar and salt in a 1-quart saucepan. Add the lime juice and slightly beaten egg yolks and mix well. Cook over medium heat, stirring constantly, until mixture coats a spoon. Add the lime rind and cool. Beat the egg whites, water and dry milk in a small mixing bowl with electric mixer at high speed until stiff peaks form. Fold in lime mixture and enough food coloring for green tinge. Reserve 1/4 cup blueberry mixture for garnish. Place 2 tablespoons remaining blueberry mixture in each tart shell and fill each tart with 1/2 cup lime mixture. Garnish with reserved blueberry mixture and chill until firm. 8 servings.

SUGARPLUM TARTLETS

1 pkg. cream cheese, softened	1/4 c. sugar
1/2 c. butter or margarine, softened	1 tsp. sherry
1 c. sifted flour	1/4 tsp. vanilla
1 1-lb. can plums	1/2 c. orange juice
1 egg	

Blend the cream cheese with butter in a mixing bowl, then stir in flour. Chill for 20 minutes. Roll out on a lightly floured board and cut out circles to fit 1 3/4-inch muffin cups. Press circles into cups. Drain the plums and cut into halves. Remove pits. Place 1 plum half in each muffin cup. Beat the egg in a bowl until frothy, then add 3 tablespoons sugar, sherry, vanilla and orange juice. Pour into muffin cups almost to top and sprinkle with remaining sugar. Bake at 325 degrees for 30 minutes or until set. Remove from pans carefully and cool. May be served warm or chilled. 6 servings.

Mrs. Joseph F. Lombardi, Panama City, Florida

WALNUT-MAPLE TARTS

1/2 c. butter	1 1/4 c. chopped walnuts
3/4 c. (firmly packed) light brown sugar	1/2 tsp. vanilla
1/2 c. maple syrup	8 unbaked tart shells
3 eggs, lightly beaten	Whipped cream
1/4 c. heavy cream	8 walnut halves

Mix the butter with brown sugar and maple syrup in a saucepan and bring to boiling point. Mix the eggs, cream, chopped walnuts and vanilla in a bowl and stir in the hot sugar mixture gradually. Pour into tart shells. Bake at 375 degrees for 20 minutes or until golden brown and custard is set, then cool. Garnish with whipped cream and with walnut halves.

COCONUT TARTS

1 recipe pie pastry	**4 tsp. lemon juice**
3 beaten eggs	**1 tsp. vanilla**
1 1/2 c. sugar	**1 3 1/2-oz. can flaked coconut**
1/2 c. melted butter or margarine	

Roll pastry 1/8 inch thick on a floured surface and cut into eight 6-inch circles. Line 2 3/4 x 1 1/4-inch muffin cups with pastry. Combine the eggs, sugar, butter, lemon juice and vanilla in a bowl and stir in coconut. Pour into pastry shells. Bake in 350-degree oven for 40 minutes or until knife inserted in center comes out clean. Cool.

Mrs. Lloyd Cherry, San Antonio, Texas

PECAN DELIGHT

1 stick butter	**1 tbsp. sugar**
1 sm. package cream cheese	**Pinch of salt**
1 c. flour	

Beat the butter with cream cheese in a bowl until fluffy. Add the flour, sugar and salt and mix well. Shape into small balls and press into muffin tins.

Pecan Filling

2 tbsp. melted butter	**1 tbsp. vanilla**
1 1/2 c. (packed) light brown sugar	**1 c. chopped pecans**
2 eggs, slightly beaten	

Pour the butter over brown sugar in a mixing bowl. Add the eggs, vanilla and pecans and mix well. Pour into pastry in muffin tins. Bake at 350 degrees for 15 minutes. Reduce temperature to 250 degrees and bake for 15 minutes longer. 12 servings.

Mrs. Paul Stone, Carlisle, Kentucky

LEMON TARTS

3 c. sifted flour	**1/2 c. lemon juice**
1 1/2 tsp. salt	**2 c. sugar**
1 c. shortening	**1 c. butter**
6 tbsp. cold water	**4 eggs, well beaten**
Grated rind of 2 lemons	**Whipped cream**

Sift the flour with salt into a bowl and cut in shortening. Add the water and mix well. Press into muffin cups. Bake at 450 degrees for 15 to 20 minutes. Combine the lemon rind, lemon juice and sugar in top of a double boiler and add butter. Cook over boiling water, stirring, until butter is melted. Stir in eggs slowly and cook, stirring, until thickened. Cool and place in tart shells. Top with whipped cream. 4 dozen.

Mrs. C. A. Ashley, Ocilla, Georgia

ALMOND BARS

1/2 c. shortening
1 1/2 c. (packed) brown sugar
1 1/8 c. flour
2 eggs
1 tsp. vanilla

1 tsp. baking powder
1/2 tsp. salt
1 c. shredded coconut
1 c. chopped almonds

Cream the shortening with 1/2 cup brown sugar in a mixing bowl. Add 1 cup flour and mix well. Spread in 8-inch square baking pan. Bake at 350 degrees for 10 minutes, then cool slightly. Beat eggs in a bowl until light. Beat in vanilla and remaining brown sugar and flour. Add remaining ingredients in order listed and blend well. Spread over baked layer. Bake for 25 minutes or until brown. Cool and cut into bars.

Eva L. Wilson, Orlando, Florida

CHRISTMAS ORANGE BARS

1 6-oz. can frozen orange juice
1/2 c. rolled oats
1/2 c. candied mixed fruit
1/2 c. chopped walnuts
1/2 c. shortening
1/2 c. sugar
1/2 c. unsulphured molasses

1 egg
2 c. sifted flour
1/4 tsp. salt
1 tsp. soda
1 tsp. ginger
1 tsp. cinnamon
1 recipe orange icing

Combine the orange juice, oats, mixed fruit and walnuts. Cream the shortening and sugar in a bowl and add molasses and egg. Mix well. Sift the flour, salt, soda and spices together and stir into molasses mixture. Add oats mixture and blend well. Pour into a greased 13 x 9-inch pan and spread evenly. Bake at 325 degrees for 40 minutes, then cool. Frost with orange icing and cut into bars. 36 bars.

Mrs. Sidney Ingram, Statesville, North Carolina

MUDHENS

1/2 c. butter or margarine
1 c. sugar
2 eggs
1 1/2 c. flour
1 tsp. baking powder

1/2 tsp. salt
1/2 tsp. vanilla
1 c. chopped nuts
1 c. (packed) brown sugar

Cream the butter and sugar in a bowl. Add 1 egg and 1 egg yolk and mix well. Sift the flour with baking powder and salt and stir into the creamed mixture. Add vanilla and mix well. Spread in a greased 9 x 13-inch pan and sprinkle with nuts. Beat remaining egg white until frothy. Add brown sugar gradually and beat until stiff. Spread over nuts. Bake at 350 degrees for 30 minutes or until done and cut into bars.

Mrs. H. C. May, Jr., Whitehaven, Tennessee

SUNSHINE DREAM BARS

1 c. sifted all-purpose flour	1 8-oz. package cream cheese
2/3 c. sugar	2 eggs
1 tbsp. grated lemon rind	2 tbsp. lemon juice
1/4 c. butter	

Sift the flour with 1/3 cup sugar into a bowl and stir in 2 teaspoons lemon rind. Cut in the butter and 1/4 cup cream cheese until particles are fine. Press into well-greased 9 x 13-inch shallow baking pan. Bake at 350 degrees for 12 to 15 minutes or until golden brown. Cream remaining cream cheese with remaining sugar in a bowl until smooth. Blend in the eggs, one at a time. Blend in remaining lemon rind and lemon juice and spread over baked mixture.

Golden Nut Topping

2 eggs	1 tsp. baking powder
1 tsp. vanilla	1/2 tsp. salt
1 c. (firmly packed) brown sugar	1 c. chopped walnuts
2 tbsp. all-purpose flour	

Beat the eggs with vanilla in a bowl until foamy. Add brown sugar gradually and beat well. Sift the flour with baking powder and salt and stir into egg mixture. Stir in 3/4 cup walnuts and spoon over cream cheese mixture. Sprinkle with remaining walnuts. Bake at 350 degrees for 25 to 30 minutes. Cool and cut into bars with a damp knife. Sprinkle with powdered sugar before serving, if desired. 3 dozen.

ICEBOX COOKIES

1 1/2 c. shortening	2 tsp. baking powder
1/3 c. sugar	4 c. all-purpose flour
1 c. (packed) brown sugar	2 tsp. vanilla
3 eggs	2 sq. chocolate, melted
1/2 tsp. soda	1/2 c. grated coconut
2 tsp. cinnamon	1/2 c. chopped nuts
1 tsp. salt	

Cream the shortening in a bowl. Add sugars gradually and beat well. Add eggs, one at a time, beating well after each addition. Sift soda, cinnamon, salt, baking powder and flour together and add to creamed mixture. Stir in vanilla and divide into 3 portions. Add melted chocolate to 1 portion, grated coconut to 1 portion and nuts to remaining portion. Shape each portion into a roll and wrap in waxed paper. Refrigerate until chilled. Slice rolls and place on cookie sheet. Bake at 350 degrees for 10 to 12 minutes. Raisins or chopped dates may be substituted for nuts.

Mrs. Raymond Williams, Morrison, Tennessee

OLD-FASHIONED TEA CAKES

1 c. butter	1 tsp. nutmeg
1 c. sugar	3 1/2 c. flour
3 eggs	Cinnamon sugar

Cream the butter and sugar in a bowl. Add the eggs, nutmeg and flour and beat until well mixed. Shape into 3 rolls, 2 inches in diameter and wrap in waxed paper. Chill for 3 hours. Cut in 1/4-inch slices and place on a greased cookie sheet. Bake at 350 degrees for 10 minutes, then sprinkle with cinnamon sugar.

Kathryn Elwert, Wichita Falls, Texas

NO-BAKE BROWNIES

2 6-oz. packages chocolate morsels	2 c. miniature marshmallows
1 1/8 c. evaporated milk	1 c. chopped pecans
3 c. vanilla wafer crumbs	1 c. sifted powdered sugar
	1/2 tsp. salt

Place the chocolate morsels and 1 cup milk in a heavy 1-quart saucepan and cook and stir over low heat until chocolate melts. Remove from heat. Mix the vanilla wafer crumbs, marshmallows, pecans, powdered sugar and salt in a 3-quart bowl. Reserve 1/2 cup chocolate mixture for glaze. Stir remaining chocolate mixture into crumb mixture and mix well. Press into a well-greased 9-inch square pan. Stir remaining evaporated milk into the reserved chocolate mixture until smooth and spread over mixture in pan. Chill until glaze is set, then cut into 36 squares.

Mrs. S. C. Edwards, Richmond, Virginia

CHOCOLATE-FRUIT SQUARES

24 graham crackers, crushed	1 can flaked coconut
1 12-oz. package chocolate chips	2 cans sweetened condensed milk
1 1/2 c. chopped pecans	Whipped cream
1 c. crystallized mixed fruit	Maraschino cherries
2 tbsp. flour	

Mix cracker crumbs and chocolate chips in a large bowl. Mix pecans and fruit with flour, coating well, then add to crumb mixture. Add coconut and milk and mix well. Press into a greased and floured 11 x 16 x 1/2-inch cookie pan. Bake at 350 degrees for 15 minutes and cut into squares while warm. Top each serving with whipped cream and a cherry.

Mrs. J. C. Worthom, Milan, Tennessee

LEMON-DATE SQUARES

1/2 c. butter	1/2 tsp. baking powder
1 c. sugar	1/2 tsp. salt
1 1/8 c. sifted flour	1 c. flaked coconut
1 tsp. grated lemon rind	1/2 c. chopped pitted dates
2 eggs	1 tbsp. lemon juice
1/4 c. confectioners' sugar	

Cream the butter and sugar in a bowl until light and fluffy. Blend in 1 cup flour and lemon rind and press into buttered 8 x 8 x 2-inch pan. Bake at 350 degrees for 20 minutes. Beat eggs until thick and lemon colored. Add the confectioners' sugar and mix well. Blend in remaining flour, baking powder, salt, coconut, dates and lemon juice and spoon over batter mixture in pan. Bake for 25 minutes longer or until firm and brown. Cool on wire cake rack and top with lemon glaze, if desired. Cut into squares.

Mrs. J. P. Allen, Channelview, Texas

NUGGETS

3 eggs	1 tsp. cinnamon
2 c. sugar	1/2 tsp. nutmeg
2 c. flour	Pinch of salt
1 tsp. baking powder	2 c. chopped pecans
2 tbsp. cocoa	

Beat eggs well and add sugar gradually. Sift the flour, baking powder, cocoa, cinnamon, nutmeg and salt together into egg mixture and mix well. Stir in pecans and spread into well-greased and floured 9 x 13-inch baking pan. Bake at 350 degrees for 30 minutes. Cool slightly and cut into squares.

Mrs. Ruby Itz, Doss, Texas

FRUITCAKE COOKIES

1 1-lb. jar candied fruit mix	1/2 tsp. soda
1/2 c. butter	1/2 tsp. salt
1 1/2 c. (firmly packed)	1 tsp. cinnamon
brown sugar	1 tsp. cloves
3 eggs, separated	1 tsp. allspice
1 1/2 tsp. lemon juice	Dash of nutmeg
1/2 c. evaporated milk	1 1/2 c. raisins
2 c. sifted flour	2 c. chopped pecans

Preheat oven to 325 degrees. Chop the candied fruit very fine. Cream the butter well in a large bowl. Add the sugar gradually and cream until light and fluffy. Beat in the egg yolks. Combine the lemon juice and milk and add to egg mixture slowly. Reserve 1/4 cup flour. Sift remaining flour with soda, salt and spices and stir all at once into the egg mixture. Mix reserved flour with the candied fruit, raisins and pecans to coat well and add to egg mixture, stirring to blend thoroughly. Fold in stiffly beaten egg whites and drop by teaspoonfuls onto an aluminum foil-covered baking sheet. Bake for 20 to 25 minutes or until lightly browned. Remove from baking sheet immediately and cool on rack. 9 dozen.

CHOCOLATE-PEANUT TREATS

1 pkg. chocolate cake mix	1/3 c. water
1 c. chopped roasted peanuts	2 tbsp. cooking oil
1 tsp. cinnamon (opt.)	1 egg

Combine the cake mix, peanuts and cinnamon in a mixing bowl and stir in the water, oil and egg. Drop from teaspoon onto ungreased cookie sheet. Bake at 350 degrees for 10 to 12 minutes.

Mrs. Johnnie Baker, Statham, Georgia

APRICOT BALLS

2 c. dried apricots	2 c. powdered sugar
1 orange	1 c. chopped pecans
2 c. sugar	

Wash the apricots and drain. Grind the apricots and orange in a food grinder. Add the sugar and place in a double boiler. Cook until thick, stirring occasionally, then chill thoroughly. Shape into small balls and roll in powdered sugar. Roll in pecans and place on a cookie sheet. Chill for 30 minutes. One can flaked coconut may be substituted for pecans.

Mrs. Luther Gribble, Wellington, Texas

COCONUT WREATHS

1 c. butter	1/2 tsp. salt
1 c. sugar	1/2 c. ground coconut
2 beaten eggs	1/2 c. ground almonds
1 tsp. vanilla	1 c. confectioners' sugar
2 1/2 c. (scant) flour	1 tbsp. milk
2 tsp. baking powder	1 tbsp. water

Cream the butter and sugar in a bowl and stir in eggs and vanilla. Sift the flour, baking powder and salt together and stir into creamed mixture. Add the coconut and almonds and mix well. Force through a cookie press in shape of small wreaths onto a greased cookie sheet. Bake at 350 degrees until lightly browned. Combine remaining ingredients in a saucepan and bring to a boil. Cool and spread on cookies. May be sprinkled with tinted coconut or other decorations, if desired.

Mrs. C. B. Byrd, Reynolds, Georgia

COCONUT-HONEY BALLS

1 c. butter or margarine	2 c. sifted all-purpose flour
1/2 c. sugar	1 c. chopped pecans
1 tsp. vanilla	1 c. shredded coconut
1 tsp. almond extract	

Cream the butter in a bowl. Add the sugar gradually and cream well. Add the vanilla and almond extract. Add the flour, pecans and coconut and mix thoroughly. Shape into balls, using a teaspoon for each, and place on ungreased baking sheet. Bake at 350 degrees for 15 to 18 minutes or until golden brown.

Pineapple Glaze

1/2 c. honey	2 tbsp. butter
1/3 c. pineapple juice	2 tbsp. vinegar

Combine all ingredients in a saucepan and simmer for 5 minutes. Cool to lukewarm. Dip warm cookies into Pineapple Glaze and let stand for 1 hour before storing.

Mrs. Frank J. Ross, Cynthiana, Kentucky

puddings &
cream custards

Puddings and cream custards are among those desserts whose eating pleasure is matched only by their nutritional value. With a foundation of milk and eggs, these desserts stand high on the food value charts. And with their endless variety of flavors, they also stand high on your family's popularity chart!

This wonderful variety is welcomed by southern homemakers who know that custards and puddings will mix and match with every menu they plan. On steamy hot summer evenings, the thoughtful homemaker treats her family to an icy-cool, smooth custard topped with a tart fruit sauce. It may be only an illusion — but everyone feels degrees cooler! And no church supper or family reunion would be complete without an enormous banana pudding — why, it's almost a southern tradition!

Creative cooks vary puddings and custards with their favorite sauces or toppings and by doing so invent many new desserts. The most cherished recipes of such imaginative southern homemakers are brought together here for your cooking and dining pleasure. Each recipe has been painstakingly perfected by a homemaker who takes pride in serving her family and friends the very best food. With an endorsement like that, you know you can depend on these recipes to bring you accolades from everyone who dines at your table.

Puddings and custards are versatile desserts — and favorites with just about every family. They may be light as custard or rich as steamed puddings. They may be served hot, warm, or cold. Steamed puddings and baked batter puddings are best served hot or warm — they become soggy when they are cold. Souffles must be served directly from the oven or they will fall. Other puddings are best served icy cold.

The secret of successful custards and puddings lies in knowing how to handle your ingredients. Eggs, milk, sugar, and flavorings are the main ingredients of most custard and pudding recipes. Eggs are their basic foundation.

Egg cookery can be wonderfully simple to master. Remember to remove eggs from the refrigerator about one hour before you are going to prepare your

cooking methods

recipe. An hour will give the eggs a chance to come to room temperature — about 75 degrees. At room temperature, they beat up to a fuller volume and are easier to separate. Another important rule is to avoid cooking the egg-milk-sugar mixture at high temperatures. Eggs may curdle, water, or toughen at high temperatures and will not hold the volume of milk needed for a successful pudding or custard. Finally, if your recipe is one that calls for hot milk to be added to beaten eggs, add the milk very slowly and stir constantly during and after the addition.

STEAMED PUDDINGS

For richly delicious flavor, it is hard to beat a steamed pudding. These puddings are baked in molds and, as the name implies, they are cooked by steam heat. The mold you choose may be elaborately fluted or a simple coffee can. If your mold doesn't have a tightly-fitting top, secure a piece of waxed paper (plastic wraps are not suitable) over the top opening with string. This will prevent water condensation from making the top of your pudding wet.

Grease both the mold and its top generously. Prepare your recipe and pour the batter into the mold. Your mold should be one-half to two-thirds full.

In a kettle, have enough rapidly boiling water to reach about halfway up to the mold. Place a rack on the bottom of the kettle, and lower the mold onto it. Cover the lid tightly and keep the temperature high until steam begins to escape, then lower the heat. Steam your pudding for the designated time, adding more water as needed to keep it halfway up the side of the mold.

After steaming, it may be necessary to place your pudding in the oven for

96

five minutes to dry the top. Before unmolding, remove the lid (or waxed paper cover) and let the pudding rest long enough to allow the steam to escape. This will help prevent cracking when the pudding is unmolded.

CUSTARDS

There are really two kinds of custards: baked custards, cooked in the oven, and boiled custards, cooked on the top of the stove over simmering water. Like puddings, custards are a blend of eggs, sugar, milk, and flavorings. If you are using pasteurized milk, it doesn't have to be scalded, but scalding will shorten your cooking time. Scalded milk should be allowed to cool enough to keep it from curdling when added to other ingredients. If you use homogenized milk, allow ten extra minutes for cooking time. If you don't have fresh milk on hand, try using unsweetened canned milk or reconstituted powdered milk. The results are just as good.

The same rules mentioned above for egg cookery apply to custard making. Nothing can turn a would-be light and delicious custard into a tough or watery dish faster than ignoring these rules, especially the one for cooking at a low temperature.

BAKED CUSTARD

Baked custard is poured into cups and the cups are set into a pan with about one inch of water. They should be baked only until set — until knife inserted near the edge of the custard comes out clean. The center will be soft, but there is enough heat left in the custard to finish baking. If you have waited too long to test and the center also tests clean, remove the custards at once from their pan of hot water and set them into ice water to stop the cooking process. Custards should be cooled on a rack, then stored in the refrigerator until serving time.

The so-called "boiled" custard is cooked in a double boiler over simmering — not boiling — water. Boiled custard is done when the mixture coats a metal spoon.

When boiled custard tests done, remove the custard, strain to remove lumps, and continue stirring to release all steam. If the steam is allowed to remain in the custard, it may become watery. If the custard gets too hot while cooking, turn it into a chilled dish and whisk quickly to cool it off, continuing until all steam is gone.

A delightful variation of boiled custard is soft custard, a sauce-like custard used as the basis of such old-fashioned desserts as Floating Island. It can be served by itself in sherbet glasses or deep sauce dishes and garnished with a bit of whipped cream. As a sauce over fresh or cooked fruit, it provides contrast in both flavor, texture, and color. And it makes an elegant hurry-up party dessert served over ladyfingers or sponge cake and garnished with flavored whipped cream.

BIRD'S NEST PUDDING

8 tart apples	1/4 c. butter, softened
Sugar	Cream
1 qt. milk	Lemon flavoring to taste
3 tbsp. cornstarch	Nutmeg to taste
8 eggs, separated	

Peel and core the apples and place in a baking dish. Fill centers of apples with sugar. Bake at 350 degrees until tender. Pour the milk into a saucepan. Add 1 cup sugar and mix well. Bring to a boil, stirring frequently. Mix the cornstarch with a small amount of water and stir into the milk mixture. Pour into beaten egg yolks, stirring constantly, then fold in stiffly beaten egg whites. Pour over apples and bake for 1 hour longer. Blend the butter, 1 cup sugar and a small amount of cream until light. Stir in the lemon flavoring and nutmeg, then serve with pudding.

Mrs. Fannie T. Sankey, Birmingham, Alabama

ENCHANTED BANANA CREAM

1 pkg. banana instant pudding mix	2 tbsp. chopped maraschino
1 c. diced bananas	cherries
1 c. miniature marshmallows	

Prepare the pudding according to package directions. Add the bananas and marshmallows and mix well. Spoon into dessert dishes and top with cherries. Chill for 1 hour. Vanilla pudding may be substituted for banana pudding.

Ruth Ollis, Morganton, North Carolina

UNBAKED BANANA PUDDING

Vanilla wafers	1 pkg. vanilla pudding mix
Sliced bananas	

Place a layer of vanilla wafers in a dish and add a layer of bananas. Prepare the pudding mix according to package directions and pour half the pudding over bananas. Repeat layers and refrigerate until chilled.

Marie Bullard, Bennettsville, South Carolina

BANANA-COCONUT DESSERT

1/2 c. banana dessert mix	2 eggs, beaten
1/2 c. coconut dessert mix	4 c. milk
1/2 c. sugar	2 tsp. butter

Mix the banana dessert mix with coconut dessert mix and sugar in top of a double boiler. Add the eggs, milk and butter and mix well. Cook over hot water for about 10 minutes or until thick, stirring constantly. Remove from heat and chill. 6-8 servings.

Christine Locklear, Pembroke, North Carolina

GINGER PUDDING

24 gingersnaps
3 c. milk
2/3 c. (packed) brown sugar

1/2 tsp. vanilla
2 well-beaten eggs

Crumble the gingersnaps into a greased baking dish. Mix the milk with brown sugar, vanilla and eggs and pour over gingersnaps. Place in pan of hot water. Bake at 350 degrees for 30 minutes or until set and serve warm with cream.

Mrs. Hilda Burdine, Somerset, Kentucky

SUMMER STRAWBERRY-BREAD PUDDING

2 pt. fresh strawberries
1 c. sugar
1/4 tsp. cinnamon
Dash of cloves
2 tbsp. water

12 slices day-old bread
1/3 c. melted butter or margarine
1 egg white, slightly beaten
2 c. sweetened whipped cream

Reserve several strawberries for garnish. Cut remaining strawberries in half and place in a saucepan. Add the sugar, spices and water and bring to a boil, stirring constantly. Reduce heat and simmer for 3 to 4 minutes. Remove crusts from bread and brush bread slices on both sides with butter. Line bottom and sides of a 1 1/2-quart baking dish with bread slices and brush edges of bread with syrup from cooked strawberries. Add alternate layers of cooked strawberries and remaining bread and cover. Chill for several hours or overnight. Brush reserved strawberries with egg white and sprinkle lightly with additional sugar. Place on a rack to dry. Garnish pudding with whipped cream and frosted strawberries.

OLD-TIME BREAD PUDDING

4 slices buttered bread, toasted	1 c. evaporated milk
1/2 c. raisins	1 c. boiling water
2 eggs, lightly beaten	1 tsp. vanilla
1/2 c. sugar	1/2 tsp. cinnamon
1/8 tsp. salt	

Cut the bread into cubes and place in a greased 2-quart baking dish. Sprinkle with raisins. Mix the eggs, 1/4 cup sugar, salt, milk and water and pour over raisins. Let set for 10 minutes. Add the vanilla and stir. Sprinkle with remaining sugar and cinnamon. Bake at 350 degrees for 30 minutes or until a knife inserted in center comes out clean. Half and half may be substituted for evaporated milk.

Mrs. Myrle Stickel, Maysville, Kentucky

BOSTON BULLY PUDDING

1 c. sugar	1 tsp. vanilla
2 eggs, beaten	1 tbsp. (heaping) flour
1/2 c. melted butter	1/2 tsp. baking powder
1/2 pkg. dates, chopped	1 c. milk
1/2 c. chopped nuts	

Beat the sugar and eggs together in a bowl. Add butter, dates, nuts, vanilla, flour and baking powder and mix well. Add the milk and mix well. Pour into a greased 9-inch square baking pan. Bake at 325 degrees for 45 minutes. Raisins may be substituted for dates.

Mrs. J. Clayton Hargrove, Eatonton, Georgia

COCOA SOUFFLE

2 tbsp. melted butter	1/3 c. sugar
2 tbsp. flour	2 tbsp. hot water
3/4 c. milk	3 eggs, separated
3 tbsp. cocoa	1/2 tsp. vanilla

Mix the butter, flour and milk in a bowl. Mix the cocoa with sugar and hot water. Add to the milk mixture and beat until smooth. Stir in the beaten egg yolks and cool. Fold in stiffly beaten egg whites and vanilla and turn into a buttered 9-inch square baking dish. Bake in 350-degree oven for 25 minutes.

Mrs. C. W. Raglin, Falfurrias, Texas

BAKED GRAHAM PUDDING

5 graham crackers, crushed	1/4 c. chopped nuts
1/2 c. sugar	1/4 c. flaked coconut
1/2 c. milk	1/4 c. chopped dates
1/2 tsp. salt	1 tsp. baking powder

Mix all ingredients in order listed and pour into a greased baking dish. Bake at 325 degrees for 45 minutes. Serve with a hard sauce or whipped cream.

Mrs. Thelma Olson, Lexington, Oklahoma

STEAMED CRANBERRY PUDDING

6 tbsp. butter	1/4 tsp. salt
3/4 c. sugar	1/2 c. milk
2 eggs	2 c. cranberries
2 1/4 c. sifted all-purpose flour	1/2 c. chopped pecans
2 1/2 tsp. baking powder	Eggnog Dessert Sauce

Cream the butter and sugar in a large mixing bowl, then add eggs, one at a time. Sift the flour, baking powder and salt together and add to creamed mixture alternately with milk. Stir in the cranberries and pecans. Turn into a 6-cup greased mold and cover with foil. Press foil tightly around edges and secure with rubber band or string. Place mold on a rack in a kettle and pour enough water into kettle to come halfway up on mold. Bring water to boil and cover tightly. Reduce heat to simmer. Steam for 1 hour and 30 minutes to 2 hours or until done. Let stand for 10 minutes, then unmold. Serve with Eggnog Dessert Sauce. Pudding may be refrigerated for several days or cooled, wrapped and frozen for several months. Thaw in refrigerator, if frozen, then wrap in foil. Bake at 325 degrees for about 45 minutes. 10-12 servings.

Eggnog Dessert Sauce

1 c. butter	1 c. eggnog
1 1/2 c. sugar	1/2 tsp. rum extract

Combine the butter, sugar and eggnog in a saucepan. Cook over low heat, stirring occasionally, until heated through, then stir in rum extract. 3 cups.

CARAMEL RICE

3/4 c. dried prunes	1/4 tsp. salt
1/2 c. sugar	1 tsp. vanilla
2 eggs, well beaten	1 1/2 c. cooked rice
1 tbsp. butter	

Place the prunes in a saucepan and cover with water. Cook for 15 to 20 minutes, then drain. Remove pits and cut prunes into small pieces. Cook 1/3 cup sugar in a skillet over low heat until melted and brown, stirring constantly. Add 1/2 cup water and cook until sugar is dissolved. Stir in remaining sugar and pour into eggs slowly, beating constantly. Add butter, salt, vanilla, rice and prunes and mix well. Pour into a buttered casserole. Bake at 350 degrees for 30 minutes. Serve warm with cream, if desired. 4-6 servings.

Mrs. Earl L. Faulkenberry, Lancaster, South Carolina

DATE-RICE PUDDING

1/2 c. chopped sugar-coated dates	1/8 tsp. salt
2/3 c. diluted evaporated milk	1 tsp. vanilla
3/4 c. cooked rice	1 tbsp. sugar
1/4 c. maple syrup	Cinnamon sugar
1 egg, separated	

Place the dates, milk and rice in top of a double boiler. Beat syrup into egg yolk and add salt and vanilla. Stir into rice mixture. Cook over boiling water for 5 to 6 minutes or until thickened, stirring frequently. Place over cold water until cool. Beat egg white with sugar until stiff and fold into pudding. Sprinkle cinnamon sugar over pudding and serve with ice cream, if desired.

Mrs. Robert L. Eddy, Sarasota, Florida

HAWAIIAN DREAM DESSERT

1 pkg. vanilla tapioca pudding	1/3 c. (packed) brown sugar
1 sm. can sliced pineapple	1/4 c. flaked coconut
2 tbsp. butter	

Prepare pudding according to package directions, then cool for 15 minutes. Stir well and spoon into 4 dessert dishes. Chill. Drain the pineapple, reserving 1/3 cup juice, and cut slices in half. Melt the butter in a skillet. Add sugar, stirring until softened, then add reserved pineapple juice gradually, stirring constantly. Add pineapple and coconut and bring to a boil. Reduce heat and simmer for 4 minutes. Serve hot over pudding. 4 servings.

Mrs. George W. Harmon, Jr., Church Hill, Tennessee

CHRISTMAS PUDDING

1/3 c. shortening	1/2 tsp. baking powder
2/3 c. (packed) brown sugar	1/2 tsp. cinnamon
2 eggs, beaten	1/2 tsp. allspice
1 c. sifted flour	1/2 tsp. cloves

1/2 c. chopped candied cherries	1/2 c. chopped nuts
1/4 c. chopped candied citron	1 tsp. vanilla
1/2 c. raisins	1/4 c. milk

Cream the shortening and sugar in a bowl. Add the eggs and beat well. Sift dry ingredients together and stir into creamed mixture. Add fruits, nuts, vanilla and milk and mix well. Pour into a well-greased casserole. Bake at 300 degrees for about 1 hour. Serve hot or cold.

Mrs. L. D. Breedlove, Walnut Grove, Mississippi

CHOCOLATE-VANILLA PUDDING

1 6-oz. package semisweet chocolate pieces	1 egg
2 tbsp. sugar	1 tsp. vanilla
Pinch of salt	3/4 c. milk
	1 pkg. vanilla pudding mix

Place all ingredients except milk and pudding mix in an electric blender container. Heat the milk in a saucepan to boiling point and pour into blender container. Cover and blend for 1 minute. Cool. Prepare the pudding mix according to package directions and cool. Place 1/2 of the chocolate mixture in 4 parfait glasses and add 1/2 of the vanilla pudding. Add remaining chocolate mixture, then add remaining vanilla pudding. Chill. Garnish with whipped cream, if desired.

PRUNE PUDDING

18 prunes
4 egg whites

1/2 c. sugar

Cook the prunes in a small amount of water in a saucepan until tender. Cool and remove pits. Mash prunes. Beat the egg whites until stiff, adding sugar gradually. Fold in prunes. Pour into greased coffee cans and cover with lids. Place in a kettle of boiling water and place weights on cans to keep submerged in water. Simmer for 1 hour. Chill and serve with whipped cream.

Emma B. Brasseaux, St. Francisville, Louisiana

PUMPKIN CHIFFON PUDDING

1 c. sugar
2 tbsp. margarine
2 eggs, separated
2 tbsp. flour

3 c. cooked mashed pumpkin
1 tsp. vanilla
1/2 c. grated fresh coconut

Cream the sugar, margarine and egg yolks in a bowl. Add the flour, pumpkin and vanilla and mix well. Beat egg whites until stiff and fold into pumpkin mixture. Pour into a 9-inch baking dish and sprinkle with coconut. Bake at 350 degrees for 30 minutes. 6 servings.

Mrs. Henry Turner, Rose Hill, North Carolina

QUEEN'S PUDDING

2 c. bread crumbs
1/2 c. sugar
Grated rind of 1 lemon
1 tbsp. butter

2 c. milk, scalded
3 eggs, separated
1 sm. jar raspberry jam or jelly

Mix the bread crumbs, 1/4 cup sugar, lemon rind and butter in a bowl. Stir in the milk, then cool for several minutes. Stir in beaten egg yolks and pour into a greased shallow baking dish. Bake in 375-degree oven for about 10 minutes. Spread jam over top. Beat egg whites until stiff but not dry and spread over jam. Sprinkle with remaining sugar and bake until meringue is lightly browned. Serve hot or cold. 6 servings.

Isla C. Painter, Stanley, North Carolina

STRAWBERRY PUDDING

2 eggs
1/4 lb. butter or margarine
1 1/2 c. confectioners' sugar

1 lb. vanilla wafers, crushed
1 qt. strawberries, sliced
1 carton dessert topping

Cream the eggs, butter and sugar in a bowl. Place 3/4 of the wafer crumbs in a casserole. Add the creamed mixture, then add strawberries. Cover with dessert topping and top with remaining wafer crumbs. Refrigerate overnight.

Mrs. H. R. Willis, Ferrum, Virginia

DANISH RUM PUDDING

1 tbsp. unflavored gelatin	1 tbsp. cornstarch
1/4 c. water	1 tsp. rum extract
2 c. eggnog	1 c. whipping cream
1/3 c. sugar	

Soften the gelatin in water. Heat eggnog in a saucepan. Mix the sugar and cornstarch and stir into eggnog. Cook, stirring constantly, until thickened. Remove from heat and stir in gelatin until dissolved. Cool. Blend in rum extract. Beat whipping cream until stiff and fold in eggnog mixture. Pour into 6 custard cups. Chill for several hours or overnight.

Raspberry Sauce

1 10-oz. package frozen raspberries	1 tbsp. cornstarch
	1 tbsp. butter
1/2 c. currant jelly	3/4 c. orange juice

Thaw the raspberries. Mix 3/4 cup raspberries and jelly in a saucepan and bring to a boil. Reduce heat. Mix cornstarch with remaining raspberries and stir into hot raspberry mixture. Cook, stirring constantly, until thickened. Remove from heat and stir in butter until melted. Cool. Stir in the orange juice and chill. Unmold pudding and top with sauce.

Mrs. W. C. Lumpkin, Tuskegee, Alabama

RASPBERRY TRIFLE

2 c. raspberries	Pinch of salt
1/2 c. sugar	1/2 c. milk
1 c. flour	1 egg, beaten
1 1/4 tsp. baking powder	2 tbsp. melted butter

Place the raspberries in a greased baking dish and sprinkle with sugar. Sift the flour with baking powder and salt into a mixing bowl. Add the milk, egg and butter and mix well. Pour over raspberries. Bake at 350 degrees for 30 minutes.

Mrs. Ralph D. McCoy, Sr., Elkton, Virginia

CRUSTY LEMON PUDDING

1 c. sugar	Grated rind of 1 lemon
3 tbsp. margarine	Juice of 1 lemon
2 tbsp. flour	1 c. milk
2 tbsp. wheat germ	1/2 tsp. vanilla
2 eggs, separated	

Cream the sugar and margarine in a mixing bowl. Add the flour, wheat germ, beaten egg yolks, lemon rind, lemon juice, milk and vanilla and mix well. Fold in stiffly beaten egg whites and pour into a baking dish. Place in a pan of hot water. Bake at 325 degrees for about 1 hour.

Mrs. John Collins, Headrick, Oklahoma

ALMOND CUSTARD WITH CRANBERRY SAUCE

1/2 c. sugar	4 eggs, beaten
1/4 tsp. salt	4 c. milk
2 1/2 tbsp. cornstarch	1 tsp. almond extract

Mix the sugar, salt and cornstarch in a saucepan and stir in the eggs. Stir in the milk gradually. Cook over low heat, stirring constantly, until mixture coats a spoon. Remove from heat and cover to prevent a skim from forming. Cool. Stir in almond extract and pour into sherbet glasses. Chill.

Cranberry Sauce

1 c. sugar	2 c. cranberry juice cocktail
1/4 c. cornstarch	1/4 c. slivered toasted almonds

Mix the sugar and cornstarch in a saucepan and stir in cranberry juice gradually. Cook over low heat, stirring constantly, until thickened. Cool slightly. Sprinkle custard with almonds and pour warm cranberry sauce over pudding.

Photograph for this recipe on page 94.

ALMOND FLAN

4 c. milk	1/4 c. cornflour
1 c. sugar	Cold milk
1/2 c. sliced blanched almonds	5 eggs, separated
1/4 c. butter	1 tsp. rum extract

Combine first 4 ingredients in a double boiler and cook until heated through. Mix the cornflour with a small amount of cold milk and stir into the almond mixture. Cook, stirring constantly, until thickened. Stir a small amount of the hot mixture into the beaten egg yolks, then stir back into the hot mixture. Cook for 2 minutes, stirring constantly, and add the rum extract. Remove from heat and cool. Fold in the stiffly beaten egg whites and refrigerate overnight.

Fruit Sauce

1 c. currant or raspberry juice	1 tbsp. sweet white wine
1/2 c. water	Sugar to taste
1 tbsp. cornflour	

Combine the first 3 ingredients in a saucepan. Bring to a boil, stirring constantly, and cook for 3 minutes. Remove from heat and add the wine and sugar. Serve warm over the Almond Flan.

Mrs. Rozanna Vachon, Dallas, Texas

ALMOND CUSTARD

1 1/2 c. sugar	4 c. milk
1/2 c. butter	1/4 tsp. salt
4 eggs, separated	1 tsp. almond flavoring
2 tbsp. flour	1/2 c. chopped toasted almonds

Cream the sugar, butter, egg yolks and flour in a bowl. Add the milk, salt and almond flavoring and mix until smooth. Fold in the stiffly beaten egg whites. Pour into a buttered baking dish and set in a pan of hot water. Bake at 350 degrees for 40 minutes or until done, then sprinkle with almonds.

Mrs. Frank Tuttle, Germanton, North Carolina

CLASSIC BOILED CUSTARD

3/4 c. sugar	2 c. milk
Pinch of salt	4 eggs, separated
2 1/2 tbsp. flour	1 tsp. vanilla

Combine the sugar, salt and flour in a saucepan and stir in milk slowly. Stir in beaten egg yolks. Cook, stirring constantly, until slightly thickened. Pour into stiffly beaten egg whites slowly, beating constantly. Stir in vanilla and chill.

Mrs. James E. Little, Johnson City, Tennessee

COFFEE CUSTARD WITH MERINGUE

3 eggs	1 c. coffee
1/2 c. sugar	1 tsp. vanilla
1/4 c. evaporated skimmed milk	

Place 1 egg and 2 egg yolks in a heavy 2-quart saucepan and beat slightly. Stir in 1/4 cup sugar, then stir in milk and coffee gradually. Cook over low heat, stirring constantly, until mixture coats a spoon. Remove from heat and stir in vanilla. Chill. Beat the egg whites in a 1 1/2-quart bowl with electric mixer at high speed until foamy. Beat in remaining sugar gradually, then beat until stiff and glossy. Shape into 6 mounds on a greased cookie sheet. Bake in 275-degree oven for 20 minutes or until set but not brown. Pour custard into shallow serving dish and float meringue mounds on top. 6 servings.

DATE FLUFF

1/4 c. instant flour	1/4 c. lemon juice
1 c. sugar	1 1/2 c. milk
1/8 tsp. salt	3 eggs, separated
1 tbsp. grated lemon rind	1/2 c. chopped dates

Combine the flour, sugar, salt, lemon rind, lemon juice, milk and egg yolks in a bowl and mix until blended. Beat egg whites until stiff and fold into egg yolk mixture. Fold in dates. Pour into a greased 9-inch square pan and place in pan of hot water. Bake at 325 degrees for 45 minutes and serve warm or cold. 6 servings.

Mrs. Jewell Hughes, Dawson, Alabama

LEMON SPONGE CUSTARD

1 1/2 c. sugar	Juice of 1 lemon
6 tbsp. butter	1 tsp. grated lemon rind
6 tbsp. flour	2 c. milk
4 eggs, separated	

Cream the sugar and butter in a bowl. Add the flour and mix well. Add the beaten egg yolks, lemon juice, grated rind and milk and mix well. Fold in beaten egg whites and pour into a greased and floured 8-inch square pan. Place in a pan of warm water. Bake at 325 degrees for 50 minutes to 1 hour or until golden brown. Cool in the pan for at least 1 hour, then invert onto serving plate. 6-8 servings.

Mrs. George W. Morrison, Jefferson, Maryland

FLAN DE POIRE

3/4 c. cooked rice	2 eggs, lightly beaten
2 c. milk	1 tsp. vanilla
1/2 c. sugar	6 canned pear halves
1/2 tsp. cinnamon	6 maraschino cherries

Mix the rice and milk in a heavy saucepan and heat until milk is scalded. Mix the sugar and cinnamon in a bowl. Add eggs and mix well. Add rice mixture gradually, stirring constantly, then stir in vanilla. Spoon into custard cups. Place pears, cut side up, in cups and place a cherry in center of each pear. Place cups in pan of hot water. Bake at 350 degrees for 30 to 40 minutes or until done. Remove cups from water and cool on rack. Chill.

Mrs. Roger P. Wolfe, Winston-Salem, North Carolina

GRAHAM-MARSHMALLOW CUSTARD

3 lge. honey graham crackers	Dash of salt
1 1/2 c. milk, scalded	1/2 tsp. vanilla
2 beaten eggs	8 quartered marshmallows
3 tbsp. sugar	

Crumble the graham crackers and place in a mixing bowl. Pour milk over cracker crumbs. Mix the eggs, sugar, salt and vanilla and stir into milk mixture slowly. Fold in marshmallows. Pour into 6 buttered ramekins or a baking dish and place in pan of hot water. Bake at 350 degrees for 15 minutes or until firm and serve warm or cold.

Mrs. G. O. Timberlake, Atlanta, Georgia

VELVET CREAM CUSTARD

1 qt. milk	1 tbsp. (heaping) flour
2 egg yolks	Vanilla to taste
6 tbsp. sugar	

Heat the milk in a double boiler until scalded. Beat the egg yolks until light. Add sugar and flour and mix until smooth. Stir in 1 cup hot milk slowly. Stir back into milk and cook, stirring constantly, until mixture coats a spoon. Add vanilla and chill. Top with whipped cream, if desired.

Mrs. Ruby L. Amberson, Morganfield, Kentucky

CUP CUSTARD JUBILEE

2 eggs, slightly beaten	1/3 c. sugar
1 c. evaporated skimmed milk	1 1/2 tsp. vanilla
2/3 c. water	Dash of salt

Preheat oven to 350 degrees. Place all ingredients in a 1-quart bowl and mix well. Pour into 4 custard cups and place cups in a shallow pan holding 1 inch of hot water. Bake for 50 minutes or until knife inserted near edge of custard comes out clean. Cool, then unmold.

frozen desserts

Show any southerner an ice cream freezer and he'll respond with a rich potpourri of memories about cranking the family's freezer on a long, languid summer afternoon. Remember the excitement of feeling the liquid cream turn into solid ice cream?Nothing ever tasted quite as good as ice cream you made yourself! But as much as southerners love their homemade ice cream, they also appreciate the many delightful frozen desserts.

And there are many! Through generations of satisfying appetites jaded by the sultry heat, southern homemakers have invented an amazing variety of frozen dessert recipes. Some are light as air — the fruit-flavored sherbets, for example. Others, like Baked Alaska, are the height of lavish elegance. Between these two lies a wonderful world of frozen desserts: ice creams . . . bombes . . . mousses . . . freezes . . . these are just a few of the many flavor treats so well represented in the sparkling section that follows.

Some of these recipes are party-special enough to highlight your next important gathering. Others are just right for at-home snacking. And all share one quality — they have been tested in homes just like yours and have won the approval of both family and friends.

The next time your family's appetite sags, try one of these melt-in-your-mouth treats. The desserts will be cool — but the words of praise will be warm!

From the elegance of a Baked Alaska to the unforgettable goodness of homemade ice cream, frozen desserts bring an air of festivity to every meal.

What are frozen desserts? First, there are mousses and parfaits. A mousse is sweetened and flavored whipped cream which has been packed into a mold and frozen without stirring. When gelatin is used in a mousse to give it body, it becomes a frozen souffle. Mousses often are flavored with chocolate, coffee, or fruit. A parfait is prepared by beating either egg yolks or whites and then pouring a hot, thick syrup over the beaten eggs. Whipped cream is added, and the mixture is packed and frozen without stirring.

Then, there are the ices, sherbets, and bombes. An ice is a fruit juice which has been sweetened with sugar and diluted with water, then frozen. Sherbet combines egg white with an ice, and milk is substituted for water. A bombe

cooking methods

FOR FROZEN DESSERTS

is a mixture of two or more frozen desserts — such as a sherbet and an ice — packed in layers in a covered mold.

Finally, there are the much-beloved ice creams. Plain (Philadelphia) ice cream is made from cream or cream diluted with milk. The cream is sweetened, flavored, and frozen. Bisque ice cream is plain ice cream which has had its texture changed by the addition of crushed macaroons, ground nuts, or sponge cake crumbs. French and American ice creams are both made from a custard base — a base which combines cream, milk, eggs, sugar, and flavorings. The mixture is combined, cooked, and frozen. French ice creams are richer in eggs than the American variations.

Ice creams are most often prepared in an ice cream freezer. But if you prefer not to use a freezer to make your ice cream, many recipes can be made in the freezing compartment of your refrigerator. The basis for these recipes is usually evaporated milk. Before adding it to other ingredients, it should be whipped just until stiff. Add milk to other ingredients as quickly as possible to keep bubbles from breaking down. Pour mixture into container and cover. Allow to freeze for two to four hours.

Homemade ice cream from your very own ice cream freezer — what fun for adults and children alike! There are two types of freezers — electric and hand operated. The difference lies in the method of operation — the steps in making ice cream are the same for both.

Chill the ice cream mixture thoroughly. If the freezer can fit into the refrigerator, the mixture should be chilled right in the freezer can. Fill it only two-thirds full. Air will be beaten into the ice cream mixture as the freezer's dasher turns, and the volume will increase by about one-third. The extra space allows for this overrun.

Ice cream salt is a must in making your own ice cream. It reduces the temperature of the ice and helps absorb the heat from the mixture being frozen. Use eight parts of ice to one part of salt for the ice cream making process. If you use small pieces of ice, it will hasten the freezing process.

If you are using a hand-operated freezer, begin to turn the handle with a slow motion. After some time the handle will be harder to turn. When this happens, turn it faster — the result will be a much smoother ice cream. If your freezer is electric, follow the manufacturer's directions.

When the ice cream is ready for freezing, drain the water from the freezer container. Be careful not to let salty ice water into the ice cream. Take the freezer can from the freezer and remove the dasher, scraping ice cream back into the can. Put two layers of waxed paper over the freezer can. Replace the lid and plug the dasher hole with a "cork" of waxed paper.

Replace the freezer can in the freezer, and surround it with a mixture of four parts ice to one part salt. In about two hours, the ice cream will harden.

Ice cream is ready for molding when its appearance is dull, it sticks to the spoon, and holds its own shape. Chill the mold thoroughly. Pack the ice cream into it, filling all corners and curves and forcing out all air. Put the mold cover on and place in the refrigerator freezing compartment to harden. To unmold a frozen dessert, remove the mold from freezer and rinse it quickly with cold water. Break the seal and remove the cover. Run a knife around the edge at a depth of about one-half an inch. Invert the mold on a serving platter and let it stand for several minutes. If the dessert doesn't come out easily, wet a cloth with lukewarm water and wring it almost dry. Then wipe the outside of the mold quickly with the cloth.

To make your frozen desserts the best ever, here are a few tried-and-proven hints.

Use more flavoring in frozen desserts than you would in unfrozen ones. The freezing process may diminish the impact of flavorings.

If you are using fruit, crush it or put it through a food chopper. Nothing spoils the smoothly delicious taste of a frozen dessert more than biting down on a big chunk of icy fruit!

Partially freeze the dessert before adding fruit. Otherwise the fruit may settle to the bottom and its juices may curdle the milk and cream in the dessert.

Scalded milk or cream will produce greater body and smoother texture in ice cream. If cream is to be whipped, whip it only to soft peaks, not stiff. Cream whipped too stiff brings a "buttery" flavor to frozen desserts and cuts down on their volume. Never fold whipped cream or whipped evaporated milk into a warm mixture — it should be either well chilled or partially frozen.

FROZEN APPLE SOUFFLE

4 egg yolks	2 c. canned applesauce
1 c. sugar	1 tsp. vanilla
1 env. unflavored gelatin	2 c. heavy cream
1/8 tsp. salt	Stemmed cherries (opt.)
1 c. light cream	Walnuts or pecans (opt.)

Beat the egg yolks in top of a double boiler over hot water until light. Mix the sugar with gelatin and salt and beat into egg yolks gradually. Mix the light cream and applesauce in a saucepan and heat through. Add to egg mixture gradually, stirring constantly, then cook, stirring, until mixture coats a spoon. Empty water from bottom of double boiler and fill with ice cubes. Place top of double boiler over ice and cool, stirring custard frequently. Add vanilla to heavy cream in a mixing bowl and whip until stiff. Fold in apple custard and turn into a 1-quart souffle dish with 3-inch band of foil tied around outside top. Freeze overnight. Apple mixture may be left in mixing bowl and chilled, folding at intervals, until thick, if mixture is not thick before turning into souffle dish. Freeze as directed. Garnish with cherries and walnuts. 6-8 servings.

APRICOT ANGEL CREAM

1 c. cooked sieved dried apricots	1 tsp. unflavored gelatin
2/3 c. sugar	1 c. heavy cream, whipped
Grated rind of 1/2 lemon	

Combine the apricots, sugar and lemon rind in a bowl and mix well. Soften the gelatin in 1/4 cup water and dissolve over hot water. Stir into the apricot mixture. Pour into refrigerator tray and chill until slightly thickened. Beat until light, then fold in whipped cream. Freeze until firm. 6 servings.

Mae A. Edwards, Prospect, Kentucky

BANANA POPSICLES

Firm ripe bananas   Chopped salted peanuts
Honey

Cut bananas in half crosswise and insert a popsicle stick into the cut surface. Roll bananas in honey until coated. Roll in peanuts and place on a cookie sheet. Freeze until solid. Store in a covered freezer container until served.

Donald H. Harris, De Funiak Springs, Florida

SNOWBALLS A MIETTE

Vanilla ice cream   3 bananas
Graham cracker crumbs   Lemon juice

Dip rounded scoops of vanilla ice cream in graham cracker crumbs and place in each dessert dish. Cut bananas in 1-inch slices and dip in lemon juice. Roll in graham cracker crumbs. Place 4 to 6 banana slices beside each ice cream ball. Serve immediately.

Mrs. E. E. Bradford, Stephenville, Texas

CHERRY BISQUE

2 egg whites   1/4 c. toasted chopped almonds
2 tbsp. sugar   1/2 tsp. vanilla
1 1/3 c. malted cereal granules 1 c. heavy cream, whipped
1/4 c. quartered maraschino   1/4 c. sifted powdered sugar
  cherries

Beat egg whites in a bowl until foamy. Add sugar gradually, then beat until stiff. Fold in 1/3 cup cereal granules, almonds, cherries and vanilla. Fold in whipped cream and powdered sugar. Sprinkle remaining cereal granules into a 9-inch square pan and pour the cherry mixture over the cereal granules. Freeze.

Mrs. Clark Hall, Tulia, Texas

BISQUE CREAM

1 env. unflavored gelatin   1 c. crushed pineapple
2 qt. milk   1 tbsp. vanilla
3 c. sugar   1 tbsp. lemon extract
1 qt. heavy cream, whipped   2 doz. almond macaroons, crushed

Soften the gelatin in milk in a saucepan. Heat over low heat, stirring constantly, until gelatin is dissolved. Add the sugar, whipped cream, pineapple and flavorings and mix well. Pour into freezer trays and freeze until partially frozen. Fold in the macaroon crumbs and freeze until firm.

Mrs. H. E. Daniel, Grand Ridge, Florida

ELEGANT RAINBOW ALASKA

1 1-lb. 1-oz. package pound cake mix	5 egg whites
1 pt. strawberry ice cream	1/4 tsp. cream of tartar
1 pt. vanilla ice cream	1/2 tsp. vanilla
1 1/2 pt. pistachio ice cream	2/3 c. sugar
	Flaked coconut

Mix the cake mix according to package directions and pour into 2 ungreased 8-inch layer pans. Bake according to package directions and cool. Line a deep 1 1/2-quart bowl with aluminum foil, allowing 1 inch foil to extend over edge of bowl. Soften the strawberry ice cream and spread in bottom of bowl. Freeze until hard. Pack vanilla ice cream on strawberry ice cream and freeze until firm. Top with pistachio ice cream and cover with foil. Press with hands to smooth the top and freeze until firm. Place 1 cake layer on a cookie sheet. Let bowl of ice cream stand at room temperature while preparing meringue. Combine the egg whites with cream of tartar and vanilla in a bowl and beat until soft peaks form. Add sugar gradually, beating constantly, and beat until stiff peaks form. Remove ice cream from bowl and invert onto cake layer. Remove foil from ice cream. Cover ice cream mixture completely with meringue and sprinkle with coconut. Bake in a 500-degree oven for 3 minutes or until browned. Serve at once. 10 servings.

BAKED ALASKA SHORTCUT

Sponge or pound cake	Meringue
Ice cream	

Cut the cake into thick slices and cut out center of each slice, leaving 1/2 inch on each side. Place on a cookie sheet and spoon ice cream into center of each slice of cake. Cover completely with meringue. Bake at 450 degrees until light brown and serve immediately.

Mrs. Phyllis Leonard, Galax, Virginia

FUDGY BAKED ALASKA

4 oz. unsweetened chocolate	1 tsp. vanilla
2/3 c. water	1 baked 9-in. pastry shell
1 1/2 c. sugar	1 qt. vanilla ice cream
1/8 tsp. salt	3 egg whites
6 tbsp. butter or margarine	1/8 tsp. cream of tartar

Combine the chocolate and water in a saucepan and heat over low heat, stirring, until chocolate is melted. Add 1 cup sugar and salt and cook over medium heat, stirring constantly, until sugar is dissolved. Remove from heat. Stir in butter and vanilla and cool thoroughly. Chill the pastry shell. Spoon half the ice cream into pastry shell and top with 1/2 cup fudge sauce. Freeze. Add remaining ice cream and top with 1/2 cup fudge sauce. Freeze. Beat egg whites and cream of tartar in a bowl until foamy. Beat in remaining sugar gradually, then beat until stiff. Spread over pie, sealing well around edges, and place pie on a baking sheet. Bake at 525 degrees for about 1 minute or until brown. Remove pie to a serving plate and add remaining fudge sauce. Serve immediately. 8 servings.

Mrs. Fred Jackson, Wauchula, Florida

FROZEN CHEESE-CRUMB DESSERT

12 slices zwieback	4 egg whites, stiffly beaten
1 1/8 c. sugar	1/2 pt. whipping cream, whipped
2 tbsp. butter	1/2 tsp. vanilla
10 oz. cottage cheese	1/2 tsp. almond extract
1 3-oz. package cream cheese	

Roll the zwieback into crumbs and blend in 2 tablespoons sugar and butter. Press half the mixture into a deep refrigerator tray. Cream the cottage cheese, cream cheese and remaining sugar in a bowl. Fold in egg whites, whipped cream and flavorings. Pour over crumb mixture and cover with remaining crumb mixture. Freeze. 10 servings.

Mary C. DeSpain, Hodgenville, Kentucky

COFFEE-MALLOW-CREAM DESSERT

1 tbsp. instant coffee	3 c. miniature marshmallows
Dash of salt	1/2 pt. cream, whipped

Mix the coffee, salt and marshmallows in top of a double boiler and cook over boiling water until melted, stirring constantly. Chill for 10 to 15 minutes. Fold in whipped cream and place in refrigerator tray. Freeze for 2 to 3 hours. Garnish with additional whipped cream and toasted almonds.

Mrs. Ed Kemper, Arlington, Virginia

CREAMY FROZEN FRUIT DESSERT

2 c. sour cream	1 9-oz. can crushed pineapple
2 tbsp. lemon juice	1/4 c. sliced drained cherries
3/4 c. sugar	1/4 c. chopped pecans
1/8 tsp. salt	2 bananas, sliced

Combine the sour cream, lemon juice, sugar and salt in a bowl and mix well. Drain the pineapple and stir into sugar mixture. Stir in the cherries, pecans and bananas. Pour into a mold or individual cups and freeze. Will keep in freezer for 2 weeks. 8 servings.

Mrs. Carl Manton, Kaplan, Louisiana

ANGEL CAKE WITH HEAVENLY TOPPING

1 loaf angel food cake	1/4 c. chopped pecans
Ice cream	1 c. miniature marshmallows
1 c. drained crushed pineapple	1 pkg. dessert topping mix
1 c. sliced strawberries	

Split the angel food cake and place a layer of ice cream between cake layers. Wrap in foil and freeze. Combine fruits, pecans and marshmallows in a bowl. Prepare dessert topping mix according to package directions and fold into pecan mixture. Chill for 24 hours. Spread dessert topping mixture over cake just before serving. 10 servings.

Mrs. Olive Wickham, Triadelphia, West Virginia

ICE CREAM PARTY CAKE

2 1/4 c. sifted cake flour	2 eggs, beaten
1 1/2 c. sugar	1 pt. vanilla ice cream
3 tsp. baking powder	1 pt. chocolate ice cream
1 tsp. salt	1 pt. strawberry ice cream
1/2 c. shortening	1 pt. heavy cream, whipped
1 c. milk	4 tbsp. powdered sugar
1 1/2 tsp. vanilla	

Sift the flour, sugar, baking powder and salt into a mixing bowl and cut in shortening. Add 3/4 cup milk and mix well. Add the vanilla, remaining milk and eggs and blend thoroughly. Pour into 2 greased and floured 9-inch layer pans. Bake at 350 degrees for 30 minutes. Cool, then split each layer. Spread each flavor of ice cream in a separate 9-inch layer pan and freeze. Place cake layers together with ice cream between layers, then freeze for several hours. Sweeten the whipped cream with powdered sugar and spread over the cake. Freeze. Remove from freezer about 15 minutes before serving. 12 servings.

Mrs. Billy Ray Hull, Tollesboro, Kentucky

NEAPOLITAN CAKE

1 10-inch angel food cake	1 pkg. dessert topping mix
1/2 gal. neapolitan ice cream	Red food coloring
1 c. miniature marshmallows	1 c. flaked coconut

Break the cake into chunks and place in a large mixing bowl. Add scoops of ice cream and marshmallows and mix lightly. Pack into a large springform pan and freeze. Prepare the dessert topping mix according to package directions and tint pink with food coloring. Tint the coconut pink with food coloring. Unmold frozen cake mixture and ice with dessert topping. Sprinkle with coconut and freeze. Thaw for 10 to 15 minutes before serving.

Mrs. E. C. Bassett, Troy, Alabama

ALMOND GATEAU MAGNIFIQUE

1 c. water	1 1/2 c. whipping cream
1/2 c. butter or margarine	1/4 c. powdered sugar
Pinch of salt	2 qt. cherry-vanilla ice cream
1 c. flour	1/2 c. toasted slivered almonds
4 eggs	

Combine the water, butter and salt in a saucepan and bring to a boil. Add the flour all at once. Cook over medium heat, stirring constantly, until mixture leaves side of pan and forms a ball. Remove from heat and blend in eggs, one at a time, beating vigorously after each addition. Mix until smooth and shiny. Drop from tablespoon 3 inches apart on ungreased cookie sheet, making 12 individual puffs. Mark an 8-inch circle on another cookie sheet. Place remaining mixture in pastry bag with large, plain tip and pipe onto cookie sheet, using marked circle as a guide for the inside diameter. Bake puffs and ring in 400-degree oven for 30 to 35 minutes or until golden brown and firm to the touch. Turn off heat and cool puffs and ring in oven with door ajar. Whip the cream with sugar until stiff. Split puffs and ring crosswise. Fill lower half of each puff with ice cream and replace top. Freeze. Spoon remaining ice cream onto lower half of ring and replace top. Garnish top of ring with some of the whipped cream and sprinkle with 3 tablespoons almonds. Combine remaining almonds and whipped cream and place in a bowl. Stack individual puffs in center of ring and serve at once with whipped cream mixture. 14-16 servings.

CARAMEL ICE CREAM

1/8 tsp. salt	2 c. scalded milk
4 egg yolks, slightly beaten	1 c. heavy cream
1/2 c. sugar	1 1/2 tsp. vanilla

Mix the salt, egg yolks and 1/4 cup sugar in top of a double boiler. Place remaining sugar in a skillet and cook over low heat until melted, stirring constantly. Add milk slowly and cook until sugar is dissolved. Pour into egg yolk mixture slowly. Cook over boiling water until mixture coats spoon, stirring constantly. Cool and strain. Add heavy cream and vanilla. Freeze until firm in hand freezer, using 3 parts ice and 1 part rock salt. Pack freezer, using 4 parts ice and 1 part rock salt.

Nancy Gaforth, Waterloo, Alabama

FROZEN MARASCHINO CREAM

4 eggs, separated	1 c. sweetened condensed milk
1 c. sugar	1/2 gal. milk
1/2 c. instant nonfat dry milk	1 8-oz. jar maraschino cherries

Beat egg yolks in a bowl until light. Stir in sugar, dry milk and sweetened condensed milk. Add milk and beat thoroughly. Chop the cherries and add cherries and juice to egg mixture. Fold in the stiffly beaten egg whites. Freeze in electric or hand-operated ice cream freezer according to freezer directions. 15-20 servings.

Mrs. Tillie Gandy, Weatherford, Texas

MILKY WAY ICE CREAM

8 Milky Way bars	1 1/2 c. sugar
Milk	2 tsp. vanilla
6 eggs, well beaten	2 lge. cans evaporated milk

Melt Milky Way bars in 2 cups milk in a double boiler, then cool. Mix eggs and sugar in a bowl and beat well. Add the vanilla and evaporated milk. Add Milky Way mixture and mix well. Pour into 1-gallon freezer container and add enough milk to fill container to within 2 inches of top. Mix well. Freeze according to freezer directions.

Mrs. B. B. Nelson, Eau Gallie, Florida

CHRISTMAS ICE CREAM

1/2 gal. vanilla ice cream	1/2 lb. red and green candied
1 1-lb. box coconut macaroons	cherries
3/4 c. slivered almonds	Sherry to taste

Soften the ice cream in a large bowl. Crush the macaroons and stir into ice cream. Add remaining ingredients and mix well. Place in refrigerator trays and freeze.

Mrs. W. C. Thompson, Charlotte, North Carolina

CHOCOLATE-MOCHA ICE CREAM

1 1/2 sq. chocolate	2 tbsp. instant coffee
1 c. sugar	1/4 tsp. salt
1 1/4 qt. thin cream	1 tbsp. vanilla

Melt the chocolate over hot water and add 1/2 cup sugar. Scald 2 cups cream in a saucepan over low heat, then stir into the chocolate mixture. Stir in coffee and cool. Add remaining sugar and cream and remaining ingredients and mix well. Pour into a 2-quart container and freeze until firm, stirring occasionally.

Mrs. Lillian Herman, Bay City, Texas

BANANA FREEZE

1 1/2 c. milk	1 pkg. instant banana pudding
1 1/2 c. heavy cream	

Combine the milk, 1/2 cup heavy cream and instant pudding in a bowl and beat with rotary beater for about 1 minute or until well mixed. Pour into a refrigerator tray and freeze until partially frozen. Pour into a chilled bowl and beat well. Whip remaining cream until stiff and fold into pudding mixture. Pour into refrigerator tray and freeze for 2 to 3 hours.

Mrs. Harry T. Collins, Columbia, South Carolina

GRAPE JUICE ICE CREAM

1 lge. can evaporated milk	3/4 c. sugar
1 can sweetened condensed milk	1 1/2 c. milk
Juice of 2 lge. lemons	Pinch of salt
1 1/2 c. grape juice	

Combine all ingredients in a large bowl and stir until sugar is dissolved. Chill. Freeze in a 1/2-gallon ice cream freezer according to freezer directions.

Mrs. P. T. Dix Arnold, Gainesville, Florida

FRESH PEACH ICE CREAM

4 c. cream	2 1/2 c. sugar
1 c. milk	1/4 tsp. salt
4 eggs	2 qt. mashed fresh peaches
1/2 c. sweetened condensed milk	1 pt. peach juice

Combine 2 cups cream with milk in top of a double boiler. Place over boiling water and cook until scalded. Beat eggs slightly and add sweetened condensed milk, sugar and salt. Blend in small amount of cream mixture slowly. Stir back into cream mixture and cook for 5 minutes longer or until mixture coats a spoon, stirring constantly. Stir in peaches, peach juice and remaining cream. Freeze in an ice cream freezer according to freezer directions. 1 gallon.

Mrs. Carl Weathers, Guthrie, Oklahoma

CREAMY LIME-AVOCADO ICE CREAM

2 soft avocados	**1/2 c. honey**
1/4 c. lime juice	**1/2 pt. whipping cream, whipped**

Peel the avocados and remove seeds. Place in a blender container and add the lime juice and honey. Blend until smooth and fold into whipped cream. Spoon into freezer tray and freeze for 4 hours or until firm. 1 quart.

PARTY STRAWBERRY ICE CREAM

6 egg yolks	**1 tbsp. vanilla**
2 c. sugar	**3 1/4 c. heavy cream**
1/2 tsp. salt	**2 pt. fresh strawberries**
3 c. scalded milk	**12 drops of red food coloring**

Beat egg yolks, 1 cup sugar and salt together in a bowl and stir in milk slowly. Pour into a medium saucepan and cook over medium heat, stirring constantly, until mixture coats a spoon. Remove from heat, add vanilla and cool. Stir in the cream, then chill. Place the strawberries in electric blender container and blend until liquefied. Strain to remove seeds and stir in food coloring. Stir in remaining sugar and refrigerate for several hours or until sugar is completely dissolved. Stir into the custard and pour into container of churn-type freezer. Freeze according to freezer directions. 4 quarts.

Photograph for this recipe on page 110.

RUM CUSTARD ICE CREAM

1 c. milk	1 egg, beaten
1 tsp. flour	1 tsp. rum extract
1/2 c. sugar	1/2 c. cream, whipped

Combine the milk, flour, sugar and egg in a saucepan and cook over low heat, stirring constantly, until mixture coats a spoon. Chill, then add rum extract. Fold in whipped cream and pour into a refrigerator tray. Freeze.

Mrs. Estelle Shalla, Bay City, Texas

STRAWBERRY CREME DE GLACE

1 qt. mashed strawberries	1 qt. milk
9 eggs, well beaten	1 pt. cream, whipped
2 1/2 c. (about) sugar	

Place the strawberries in a large bowl and stir in the eggs and sugar. Add the milk and mix well. Fold in the whipped cream and pour into a 1-gallon freezer container. Freeze according to freezer directions.

Mrs. Elmer Martin, Berryville, Arkansas

FRENCH VANILLA ICE CREAM

1/2 c. sugar	3 egg yolks, beaten
1/4 tsp. salt	1 tbsp. vanilla
1 c. milk	1 c. whipping cream

Combine the sugar, salt, milk and egg yolks in a saucepan. Bring to a boil over medium heat, stirring constantly, then cool. Add vanilla. Pour into a refrigerator tray and freeze until partially frozen. Whip the whipping cream until soft peaks form. Place milk mixture in a chilled bowl and beat until smooth. Fold in whipped cream and pour into 2 freezer trays. Freeze for 3 to 4 hours or until firm, stirring frequently during first hour of freezing. 1 quart.

Mrs. Margaret C. Fox, Afton, Virginia

MALLOW CREAM

30 lge. marshmallows	2 tsp. vanilla
Milk	1 can sweetened condensed milk
4 eggs, beaten	1 pt. whipping cream
1/2 c. sugar	

Melt the marshmallows in 1/2 cup milk in a saucepan over low heat and remove from heat. Mix eggs with sugar and stir into milk mixture slowly. Add the vanilla and sweetened condensed milk and pour into gallon freezer container. Add whipping cream, then add enough milk to fill freezer container to within 2 inches of top. Freeze according to freezer directions.

Mrs. Eugene Ronald, Greensburg, Kentucky

FROZEN LEMON MOUSSE

Vanilla wafer crumbs	1/2 c. lemon juice
6 eggs, separated	1/2 pt. cream, whipped
1 1/4 c. sugar	

Cover the bottom of a 9-inch square pan with wafer crumbs. Beat egg whites until stiff, adding sugar gradually. Add the egg yolks, one at a time, beating well after each addition. Add lemon juice and beat well. Fold in the whipped cream and turn into crumb-lined pan. Cover top with wafer crumbs and freeze. 12 servings.

Mrs. Virgil Hanson, Hamilton, Mississippi

FROZEN LEMON CREAM

1 c. finely crushed corn flakes	Dash of salt
1/4 c. melted butter	1/2 tsp. grated lemon rind
2 eggs, separated	1/4 c. lemon juice
1/2 c. sugar	3/4 c. whipping cream, whipped

Mix corn flake crumbs and butter and press 3/4 of the mixture firmly on the bottom and sides of refrigerator tray. Combine egg yolks and 1/4 cup sugar in top of a double boiler and mix thoroughly. Add the salt, lemon rind and lemon juice and mix well. Cook over boiling water, stirring constantly, for about 5 minutes or until slightly thickened. Cool, then fold in whipped cream. Beat egg whites until foamy. Add remaining sugar gradually and beat until stiff peaks form. Fold in cream mixture and pour into refrigerator tray. Sprinkle with remaining corn flake mixture and freeze for about 4 hours or until firm. Slice and serve. 6-8 servings.

Star Cardwell, Louisburg, North Carolina

ICE CREAM SANDWICH

3 eggs, separated	1 c. heavy cream, whipped
1/2 c. sugar	Vanilla wafer crumbs
5 tbsp. lemon juice	

Mix the egg yolks, sugar and lemon juice in a saucepan and cook over low heat until thickened, stirring constantly. Cool. Beat egg whites until stiff and fold into sugar mixture. Fold in whipped cream. Cover bottom of refrigerator tray with crumbs. Add the lemon mixture and cover with crumbs. Freeze.

Mrs. B. M. Bolinger, Vale, North Carolina

MINT FLAN

1 1/2 tsp. unflavored gelatin	6 drops of green food coloring
2 tbsp. water	1/4 tsp. salt
1/2 c. crushed white peppermint candy	6 tbsp. sugar
1/4 c. milk	1 c. heavy cream, whipped
2 eggs, separated	12 chocolate cookies, crushed

Soften the gelatin in water. Dissolve candy in milk in top of double boiler over boiling water. Beat egg yolks well, then stir in a small amount of milk mixture. Stir back into milk mixture and cook until thick, stirring constantly. Stir in food coloring. Add the gelatin and stir until dissolved. Chill until thickened. Add salt to egg whites and beat until stiff, but not dry. Add sugar gradually, beating constantly. Fold into gelatin mixture, then fold in whipped cream. Place half the cookie crumbs in 2 refrigerator trays. Pour in mint mixture and cover with remaining crumbs. Freeze for 3 to 4 hours. 8 servings.

Mrs. Margaret P. Baughcone, Inman, South Carolina

MINTED FRUIT PARFAIT

1 1/2 gal. vanilla ice milk	2 pt. whipping cream
Wintergreen oil	Sugar to taste
Green food coloring	Green maraschino cherries

Soften the ice milk in a large bowl and beat in enough wintergreen oil for desired flavor. Beat in several drops of food coloring. Beat 1 pint whipping cream until stiff and add sugar. Fold into ice cream mixture. Pour into greased mold and cover with aluminum foil. Freeze. Spoon into parfait glasses. Beat remaining cream until stiff and add sugar. Place on frozen mixture and top each serving with a cherry.

Mrs. Kenneth McDonald, Knoxville, Tennessee

ANGELICA

1 1/2 c. sugar	1 tsp. vanilla
1/2 c. water	1 1/2 pt. whipping cream
2 egg whites	Sliced sweetened strawberries

Combine the sugar and water in a saucepan and bring to a boil. Cook until syrup spins a thread. Beat egg whites in a bowl until stiff. Pour syrup into egg whites slowly, beating constantly. Cool and add vanilla. Beat the whipping cream until stiff and fold into egg white mixture. Freeze. Place alternate layers of Angelica and strawberries in parfait glasses and serve. Other fruits may be substituted for strawberries.

Mrs. L. V. Meskill, Fairfield, Alabama

HONEY PARFAIT

2 egg whites	1 c. heavy cream
Pinch of salt	1/4 tsp. almond extract
1/3 c. strained honey	Fresh sliced peaches

Beat egg whites with salt in a bowl until stiff. Add honey slowly, beating constantly. Whip cream until stiff and fold into honey mixture. Stir in almond extract. Pour into refrigerator tray and freeze. Fill parfait glasses with layers of peaches and honey cream and serve. 6 servings.

Mrs. James Fitzgerald, Danville, Virginia

STRAWBERRY-CREAM DESSERT

1 pkg. strawberry flavor whipped dessert mix	1 c. sour cream
2 tbsp. sugar	1/2 tsp. almond extract

Combine the dessert mix and sugar, then prepare according to package directions. Blend in sour cream and almond extract and spoon into a 1-quart mold. Freeze for at least 6 hours. Loosen sides of mold with a spatula and dip mold quickly into hot water. Place a moistened serving plate on top of mold. Invert mold and plate together and remove mold gently. Garnish with dollops of prepared whipped topping and maraschino cherries, if desired. 6 servings.

Photograph for this recipe on page 2.

BUTTERSCOTCH-CREAM DESSERT

1 roll butterscotch cookie mix	Caramel sauce
Vanilla ice cream, softened	Whipped cream

Bake the cookie mix according to package directions. Roll cookies into fine crumbs and line bottom of 8 x 12-inch pan with half the crumbs. Cover with a layer of ice cream and pour layer of caramel sauce over ice cream. Cover with remaining crumbs and freeze. Cut in squares and serve with whipped cream and caramel sauce.

Mrs. Gene Collins, Marvell, Arkansas

FESTIVE ICE CREAM BRICK

1 c. whipping cream	1 1/4 c. moist toasted coconut
1/4 c. sugar	9 maraschino cherries
1/2 gal. brick cherry-vanilla ice cream	6 sm. strips green citron

Combine the whipping cream and sugar in a bowl and beat until soft peaks form. Peel carton from ice cream and place ice cream on a chilled platter. Spread whipped cream over top and sides and sprinkle with coconut. Arrange cherries on top in three clusters and add citron strips to resemble leaves. Freeze until ready to serve. 10-12 servings.

Mary L. Vaughn, Dallas, Texas

SUPREME PECAN-COCONUT BARS

1 c. (packed) brown sugar	1 c. chopped pecans
1/4 lb. margarine	1 c. toasted flaked coconut
2 c. crushed corn flakes	1 qt. vanilla ice cream

Combine the brown sugar and margarine in a saucepan and boil for 1 minute. Pour over corn flake crumbs. Add pecans and coconut and mix well. Press half the mixture into a 9-inch square cake pan. Cover with ice cream and top with remaining corn flake mixture. Cover with foil and freeze. 9 servings.

Mrs. Mary Williams, Albany, Georgia

MOCHA FREEZE

1 1/2 c. graham cracker crumbs	3 egg whites, at room temp.
3/4 c. sugar	1/8 tsp. salt
1/2 c. chopped walnuts	3 tbsp. cocoa
1/4 c. soft butter or margarine	1 tsp. instant coffee
1 c. evaporated milk	

Combine cracker crumbs, 1/4 cup sugar and walnuts in a bowl. Add butter and mix well. Sprinkle 2 cups crumb mixture into waxed paper-lined 9-inch square pan and press down well. Freeze. Freeze evaporated milk in refrigerator tray until ice crystals form around edges of tray. Beat egg whites and salt until frothy and beat in remaining sugar slowly. Whip milk in a chilled bowl until stiff and add cocoa and coffee. Fold into meringue. Spread over crumb mixture and sprinkle remaining crumb mixture on top. Freeze overnight. 16-18 servings.

Mrs. George Gummelt, Hallettsville, Texas

TROPICAL FRUIT FREEZE

1/2 c. evaporated skimmed milk	1/2 tsp. grated orange rind
1 egg, separated	Dash of salt
1/2 c. sugar	2 tbsp. lemon juice
2 tbsp. orange juice	

Freeze the milk in an ice tray until ice crystals form around edges. Mix the egg yolk, sugar, orange juice, orange rind and salt in a 1-quart bowl. Pour the milk into cold, small mixing bowl and add egg white. Whip with electric mixer at high speed, using cold beaters, until fluffy. Add the lemon juice and whip until stiff. Beat in the sugar mixture gradually at low speed. Pour into a 5 1/2-cup ring mold and freeze for about 3 hours or until firm. Unmold and garnish with mandarin oranges and coconut. 4-6 servings.

PEACH MOUSSE

2 c. sliced fresh peaches	2 c. cream, whipped
2/3 c. sugar	Almond extract to taste

Cover the peaches with sugar and let stand for 1 hour. Press through a sieve. Fold in whipped cream and almond extract and pour into a mold. Freeze.

Mrs. Ila Lyell, Nortonville, Kentucky

GINGERED PEACH GLACE

1 can peach pie filling	1/2 c. chopped pecans
1 can sweetened condensed milk	2 tbsp. chopped candied ginger
1 tbsp. lemon juice	1 1/2 c. heavy cream, whipped

Combine the pie filling and milk in a bowl and beat with electric mixer until peaches are crushed. Mix in lemon juice, pecans and candied ginger, then fold in whipped cream. Pour into ice cube trays and freeze until firm. Serve in parfait glasses.

Mrs. Denver Conrad, Orma, West Virginia

FROZEN PEACH MACAROON TORTE

2 c. mashed peaches	1 c. heavy cream, whipped
1 tbsp. lemon juice	1 c. macaroon cookie crumbs
1/3 c. sugar	

Combine the peaches, lemon juice and sugar in a bowl and mix well. Fold in whipped cream. Place half the crumbs in an 8-inch baking pan. Top with peach mixture and sprinkle remaining crumbs on top. Freeze. Cut into squares to serve.

Mrs. Neil Horne, Richlands, North Carolina

GOLDEN PEACH PARFAIT

6 egg yolks	1 c. mashed peaches
1 1/4 c. sugar	1 pt. heavy cream
1/3 c. water	1/2 tsp. almond extract
Dash of salt	1/2 tsp. vanilla

Beat the egg yolks well in top of double boiler and set aside. Combine 1 cup sugar, water and salt in a 1-quart saucepan. Bring to a boil over low heat, stirring constantly, then cook, without stirring, to soft-ball stage. Beat syrup into egg yolks gradually and cook over simmering water, stirring constantly, until thickened. Cool and add peaches. Chill. Whip heavy cream until soft peaks form. Add remaining sugar gradually and beat until stiff peaks form. Fold into peach mixture and add flavorings. Turn into deep mold. Freeze for 3 to 4 hours without stirring. 8 servings.

Mrs. H. L. Crute, Radford, Virginia

PEACH MOUSSE

1 c. chopped peaches	2 egg whites, lightly beaten
6 tbsp. sugar	Dash of salt
1 c. whipping cream, whipped	

Mix peaches and 1/4 cup sugar and fold into whipped cream. Add remaining sugar and salt to egg whites and beat until soft peaks form. Fold into peach mixture and pour into molds. Freeze until firm. 6-8 servings.

Mrs. Agnes Hackley, Louisville, Kentucky

PEACH MARLOW

1 c. crushed peaches	20 marshmallows
3 tbsp. sugar	1/4 c. water
1 tbsp. lemon juice	1/2 pt. whipping cream, whipped

Sprinkle peaches with sugar and lemon juice and let stand. Combine marshmallows and water in a saucepan and cook over low heat, stirring occasionally, until melted. Add peaches and chill until thickened. Fold in whipped cream and pour into freezing tray. Freeze, without stirring, until firm. 6 servings.

Mrs. Ruby McClain, Knoxville, Tennessee

ANGEL FROST

5 c. sugar	Juice of 3 lemons
2 c. water	1 qt. canned apricots, mashed
Juice of 3 oranges	1 pt. cream

Mix the sugar and water in a saucepan and simmer for 3 to 5 minutes. Cool. Add the juices and apricots and mix well. Pour into 1-gallon freezer container and fill 3/4 full with cold water. Freeze according to freezer directions until partially frozen. Add the cream and freeze until firm.

Mrs. M. K. Carter, San Saba, Texas

PINEAPPLE SHERBET

1/2 env. unflavored gelatin	1 9-oz. can crushed pineapple
2 tbsp. cold water	1 tsp. vanilla
2 c. buttermilk	1 egg white
1 c. sugar	

Soften the gelatin in cold water and dissolve over hot water. Combine the buttermilk, 3/4 cup sugar, pineapple, vanilla and gelatin in a bowl and mix well. Pour into a refrigerator tray and freeze until firm. Place in a bowl. Break into chunks and beat until smooth. Beat egg white until soft peaks form. Add remaining sugar gradually and beat until stiff peaks form. Fold into pineapple mixture. Return to refrigerator tray and freeze until firm. 4-6 servings.

Eva J. Nance, Asheboro, North Carolina

KEY LIME SHERBET

1 pkg. lime pie filling	2 1/2 c. water
3/4 c. sugar	2 eggs, separated

Combine the pie filling and 1/2 cup sugar in a saucepan and add the water gradually. Add the lightly beaten egg yolks and stir until smooth. Bring to a boil over medium-high heat, stirring constantly. Break flavor capsule, if undissolved, and stir into filling. Remove from heat and cool slightly. Beat the egg whites in a bowl until foamy. Beat in remaining sugar gradually and beat until soft peaks form. Fold in lime mixture and pour into freezer tray. Freeze. 1 1/2 quarts.

BUTTERMILK SHERBET

1 pkg. lemon flavor whipped dessert mix	1/2 c. cold water
1 tbsp. sugar	1 tbsp. lemon juice
1 c. cold buttermilk	1 tsp. grated lemon rind

Combine the dessert mix and sugar in a deep, narrow bowl and blend in 1/2 cup buttermilk. Whip with electric mixer at highest speed for 1 minute. Mixture will be very thick. Blend in remaining buttermilk and whip at highest speed for about 2 minutes. Blend in water, lemon juice and lemon rind and pour into a shallow pan. Freeze for 4 hours or longer. Let stand at room temperature for 15 minutes, then spoon into large serving dish. Top with fresh blueberries and strawberry halves, if desired. 6 servings.

Photograph for this recipe on page 2.

GINGER ALE SHERBET

1 sm. package lemon gelatin	2 c. unsweetened pineapple juice
1 1/2 c. sugar	1 pt. ginger ale
4 tbsp. lemon juice	

Dissolve the gelatin in 1 cup hot water in a bowl. Add the sugar and stir until dissolved. Cool. Add the lemon juice, pineapple juice, 1 cup cold water and ginger ale. Freeze in ice cream freezer according to freezer directions. Remove dasher and pack. Let set for 2 to 3 hours before serving. 2 quarts.

Mrs. Frank McClaugherty, Glade Spring, Virginia

LIME SHERBET

2 marshmallows	1 tbsp. lemon juice
1 c. boiling water	1/2 tsp. green food coloring
1 c. ginger ale	2 egg whites
1/4 c. lime juice	1 tbsp. sugar

Melt the marshmallows in boiling water in a bowl. Add the ginger ale, juices and food coloring and mix well. Cool. Beat the egg white in a bowl until stiff, adding sugar gradually. Fold into the lime mixture and pour into a refrigerator tray. Freeze until firm. 8 servings.

Mrs. Tressie Halman, Chico, Texas

FRESH PEACH SHERBET

2/3 c. sweetened condensed milk	1/2 c. water
2 tbsp. lemon juice	1 c. crushed fresh peaches
2 tbsp. melted butter	2 egg whites, stiffly beaten

Blend the milk with the lemon juice, butter and water in a bowl. Add the peaches and chill. Fold in egg whites and pour into freezing tray. Freeze until partially frozen, then remove to a bowl. Beat until smooth and pour back into freezing tray. Freeze until firm. 6 servings.

Mrs. Robert Craft, Macon, Georgia

FROSTY STRAWBERRY SQUARES

1 c. sifted flour	1 c. sugar
1/4 c. (packed) brown sugar	2 c. sliced strawberries
1/2 c. chopped walnuts	2 tbsp. lemon juice
1/2 c. butter or margarine	1 c. heavy cream, whipped
2 egg whites	

Combine first 4 ingredients in a bowl and mix well. Spread in shallow baking pan. Bake at 350 degrees for 20 minutes, stirring occasionally. Sprinkle 2/3 of the flour mixture in a 13 x 9 x 2-inch baking pan. Combine the egg whites, sugar, strawberries and lemon juice in a large bowl. Beat with electric mixer at high speed for about 10 minutes or until stiff peaks form. Fold in whipped cream and spoon over flour mixture. Top with remaining flour mixture. Freeze for 6 hours or overnight, then cut into squares.

Mrs. Walter Wood, Lipscomb, Alabama

chilled desserts

Everyone uses the oven to produce great desserts – but how many of us have "cooked" in our refrigerators? The clever ladies who cook in the Southland have – with absolutely delicious results!

They have created a wide world of chilled desserts, a wonderful world that is now yours to explore in the following section. Angel cakes with rich fillings . . . lemon ice box pies . . . peach treats . . . charlottes . . . recipes for these and many other chilled desserts are the inspired creations of southern homemakers who wanted that just-right cool dessert for their families and guests. Turning to their refrigerators, they produced a group of recipes unmatched in inventiveness and variety. Some feature sweet flavors – chocolate, coffee, and peach. Others highlight the tart bite of citrus flavors. But all offer you a light and bright way to end every meal.

Each recipe you will encounter in these idea-packed pages is the invention of a southern homemaker. It has been developed and modified in her kitchen until it was the very best dish her skills could devise.

These are not ordinary recipes – they are extraordinary dishes which are served when nothing but the best will do. Somehow they manage to turn every meal into a special occasion. Try one tonight – you'll be rewarded with your family's appreciative gusto!

SNOW CAKE

2 env. unflavored gelatin	1 No. 2 can crushed pineapple
4 tbsp. cold water	Juice of 1 lemon
1 c. boiling water	3 pkg. dessert topping mix
1 c. sugar	1 lge. angel food cake
1/2 tsp. salt	1 c. flaked coconut

Soften the gelatin in cold water in a bowl. Add boiling water, sugar and salt and stir until dissolved. Add the pineapple and lemon juice and mix well. Chill until partially set. Prepare 2 packages dessert topping mix according to package directions and fold into gelatin mixture. Break the angel food cake into small pieces. Place alternate layers of cake and gelatin mixture in 13 x 9 1/2-inch pan and press down. Refrigerate overnight. Prepare remaining dessert topping mix according to package directions and spread over cake mixture. Sprinkle with coconut. 15 servings.

Mrs. Richard Quirk, Nashville, Tennessee

CHOCOLATE RAJAH

1 8-oz. angel food cake	1 pkg. chocolate instant pudding
1/2 pt. heavy cream	mix
1 c. milk	1/2 c. toasted slivered almonds

Slice the cake crosswise into 4 equal parts. Whip the cream until stiff. Add pudding mix to milk in a bowl and beat until smooth and thick. Fold half the whipped cream into pudding and spread half the mixture on 3 cake layers. Place layers together, having plain layer on top. Fold remaining whipped cream into remaining pudding mixture and spread on top and side of cake. Sprinkle almonds on top and refrigerate until chilled.

Mrs. Willie Carpenter, Graysburg, North Carolina

ANGEL CUSTARD ROYAL

6 eggs, separated	1/4 c. cold water
1 1/2 c. sugar	Yellow food coloring
3/4 c. lemon juice	1 14-oz. angel food cake
1 tbsp. unflavored gelatin	Sweetened whipped cream

Combine the egg yolks, 3/4 cup sugar and lemon juice in top of a double boiler and mix well. Cook over hot water, stirring constantly, until mixture coats a spoon. Remove from water. Soften the gelatin in cold water and stir into egg yolk mixture. Cool. Beat egg whites until stiff, adding remaining sugar gradually, then fold in several drops of food coloring. Fold into cooled mixture. Break cake into large pieces. Arrange 1/3 of the cake in a greased tube pan and pour 1/3 of the custard mixture over cake. Repeat layers twice and chill until firm. Invert onto a serving place and fill center and cover side with whipped cream. Serve immediately. 12 servings.

Mrs. Wesley L. Bonney, Norfolk, Virginia

BAVARIAN CREAM

1 3 1/4-oz. package chocolate pudding and pie filling	1 egg, slightly beaten
1/4 c. sugar	2 c. milk
1 env. unflavored gelatin	1 tsp. vanilla
Dash of salt	1 env. whipped topping mix

Combine the pudding, sugar, gelatin and salt in a saucepan. Blend the egg with milk and add to pudding mixture gradually, blending well. Bring to a full boil over medium heat, stirring constantly. Remove from heat and add the vanilla. Place waxed paper directly on surface of hot pudding and chill for at least 2 hours. Prepare whipped topping mix according to package directions. Beat pudding until creamy and blend in whipped topping. Spoon into buttered 1-quart mold and chill for at least 2 hours or until firm. Garnish with additonal whipped topping and chocolate curls, if desired. 8 servings.

CHOCOLATE-TOFFEE DESSERT

1 c. vanilla wafer crumbs	1 1/3 c. chocolate pieces, melted
2/3 c. soft butter	2/3 c. chopped walnuts
1 1/3 c. sifted confectioners' sugar	1 tsp. vanilla
2 eggs, separated	Whipped cream

Sprinkle half the crumbs in 8 x 8 x 2-inch pan. Cream the butter and confectioners' sugar in a bowl and stir in egg yolks, chocolate, walnuts and vanilla. Fold in stiffly beaten egg whites and spread over crumbs in pan. Sprinkle with remaining crumbs and chill. Cut into squares and top with whipped cream. 9-12 servings.

Mrs. Thomas H. Wolter, Decatur, Alabama

EMPRESS CHOCOLATE DESSERT

20 lge. marshmallows	1 c. whipping cream, whipped
5 chocolate-almond candy bars	1 tsp. vanilla
1/2 c. milk	1 recipe graham cracker crust

Melt the marshmallows and candy bars in milk in a double boiler, then cool. Fold in the whipped cream and vanilla. Sprinkle graham cracker crust in a 9-inch square baking dish and pour chocolate mixture over crust. Chill.

Mrs. A. J. Stafford, Limestone, Tennessee

CHOCOLATE SUNDAE PIE

1 pkg. chocolate flavor whipped dessert mix	1 baked 8-in. pie shell, cooled
1/8 tsp. mint extract (opt.)	1/2 c. semisweet chocolate chips
	2 tbsp. water

Prepare the dessert mix according to package directions and blend in mint extract. Pour into the pie shell and chill for at least 1 hour. Melt the chocolate chips in a saucepan over low heat, stirring constantly, then blend in water. Pour onto center of pie and spread to edge quickly. Chill for several minutes to set glaze. Garnish with fresh orange slices and mint leaves, if desired.

Photograph for this recipe on page 2.

CHOCOLATE SOUFFLE

2 env. unflavored gelatin	4 eggs, separated
2 c. milk	2 c. semisweet chocolate pieces
1 c. sugar	1 tsp. vanilla
1/4 tsp. salt	2 c. heavy cream, whipped

Soften the gelatin in milk in a saucepan. Add 1/2 cup sugar, salt, egg yolks and chocolate pieces and mix well. Cook over low heat, stirring constantly, until gelatin is dissolved and chocolate is melted. Remove from heat and beat with a rotary beater until chocolate is blended. Stir in vanilla. Chill, stirring occasionally, until mixture mounds slightly when dropped from a spoon. Beat egg whites until stiff but not dry, adding remaining sugar gradually, and fold into chocolate mixture. Fold in whipped cream and turn into a 2-quart souffle dish with a 2-inch collar of foil tied around outside top. Chill until firm. Remove collar and garnish with additional whipped cream and chocolate curls, if desired. 8 servings.

Mrs. M. H. Hatcher, Gray, Georgia

CHOCOLATE CREME GATEAU

1 6-oz. package chocolate pieces	1 c. heavy cream
4 eggs, separated	1 10-in. angel food cake
1/4 c. sugar	1 c. chopped nuts

Melt the chocolate in a saucepan over low heat, then cool. Beat egg yolks until light and stir into chocolate. Beat the egg whites until stiff, adding 2 tablespoons sugar gradually, and fold into chocolate mixture. Whip the cream until stiff and add remaining sugar. Fold into chocolate mixture. Place alternate layers of cake, chocolate mixture and nuts in a glass baking dish and chill for 12 hours. Cut into squares and top with additional whipped cream.

Mrs. Leon V. Smith, Brigham, Utah

BLANC MANGE SUPREME

3 tbsp. cornstarch
1/3 c. sugar
1/8 tsp. salt
3/4 c. cold milk
1 1/2 c. scalded milk

1 tsp. vanilla
1/2 c. crunchy peanut butter
1 6-oz. package semisweet chocolate chips

Mix the cornstarch, sugar and salt in top of a double boiler. Stir in 1/2 cup cold milk, then add scalded milk gradually. Cook over boiling water until thick, stirring frequently. Add the vanilla and peanut butter and blend well. Cook for 5 to 10 minutes longer. Rinse 6 individual molds with cold water and pour in the milk mixture. Chill. Melt chocolate chips over hot water and stir in remaining milk. Mix until smooth. Unmold the chilled mixture and place in dessert dishes. Spread the chocolate mixture on each serving.

Mrs. J. W. Chatham, Greenwood, Mississippi

MARYANNE

2 3-oz. packages raspberry gelatin
6 slices sponge cake

2 bananas, sliced
1 1/2 c. cream

Prepare 1 package gelatin according to package directions. Place cake slices in a 13 x 9-inch shallow pan in a single layer and pour gelatin over cake. Chill until firm. Prepare remaining gelatin according to package directions and add bananas. Chill until partially set. Add 1/2 cup cream and whip until frothy. Pour into a 13 x 9-inch pan and chill until firm. Cut cake mixture into squares and place on serving plates. Cut banana mixture into squares and place on cake squares. Whip remaining cream until stiff and place on top of gelatin squares.

Mrs. Margie North, Erick, Oklahoma

BURNT MILK

1 can sweetened condensed milk
6 oz. miniature marshmallows
1 sm. can crushed pineapple

1 c. chopped pecans
2 c. sweetened whipped cream

Place the can of milk in a saucepan and cover with water. Bring to a boil and reduce heat. Simmer for 2 hours and 30 minutes. Open can and place milk in a bowl. Add the marshmallows and stir until dissolved. Drain the pineapple and stir into milk mixture. Add the pecans and mix well. Chill overnight. Serve with whipped cream. 8 servings.

Mrs. Junior Dixon, Haskell, Oklahoma

FRESH BLUEBERRY REFRIGERATOR CAKE

1 env. unflavored gelatin	1/4 tsp. salt
1/2 c. orange juice	1 c. fresh blueberries
1/2 c. hot water	2 egg whites, stiffly beaten
1 tbsp. lemon juice	1 c. heavy cream
1/2 c. sugar	Ladyfingers

Soften the gelatin in orange juice in a bowl and stir in the hot water. Stir in the lemon juice, sugar and salt. Wash and crush the blueberries and add to gelatin mixture. Chill until thickened and fold in egg whites. Whip 1/2 cup cream until stiff and fold into the blueberry mixture. Line bottom and side of an 8-inch springform pan with ladyfingers and pour in half the blueberry mixture. Cover with layer of ladyfingers. Add remaining blueberry mixture and cover with ladyfingers. Chill until firm. Whip remaining cream until stiff and add 1 tablespoon additional sugar. Garnish the ladyfinger mixture with whipped cream and top with additional blueberries. 8 servings.

Photograph for this recipe on page 132.

AMBROSIA REFRIGERATOR CAKE

1 1/2 c. graham cracker crumbs	1 c. diced oranges
2 tbsp. sugar	1 1/2 c. shredded coconut
1/4 c. melted butter	1 lge. can evaporated milk
2 3-oz. packages orange gelatin	1/4 c. lemon juice
1 No. 2 can crushed pineapple	

Mix the crumbs, sugar and butter and press into an oblong baking pan. Place gelatin in a large mixing bowl. Place the pineapple in a saucepan and bring to a boil. Add to gelatin and stir until dissolved. Chill until thickened. Add oranges and 1 cup coconut and mix well. Freeze the evaporated milk until icy. Add the lemon juice and whip until stiff. Fold into pineapple mixture and spoon into crumb crust. Toast remaining coconut and sprinkle on top. Chill for 3 to 4 hours. 20 servings.

Mrs. W. D. Shelton, Trumann, Arkansas

HEAVENLY CAKE AND CREAM

5 eggs, separated	1 c. chopped walnuts
1 c. sugar	1 tsp. baking powder
1 c. chopped dates	2 c. sweetened whipped cream
1 c. bread crumbs	

Mix the egg yolks and sugar in a bowl and stir in dates, bread crumbs and walnuts. Fold in stiffly beaten egg whites. Sprinkle with baking powder and mix well. Turn into 2 well-greased 9-inch round layer pans. Bake at 350 degrees for 25 to 30 minutes or until done. Cool and break into pieces. Place alternate layers of cake and whipped cream in a large bowl and chill for several hours or overnight. 10 servings.

Mrs. R. R. Scheer, Virginia Beach, Virginia

MACAROON-SHERRY CREME

1 c. sugar
4 eggs, separated
1 pt. milk, scalded
1 tbsp. unflavored gelatin
1 tbsp. water

1 doz. toasted coconut macaroons
1 tsp. sherry flavoring
Whipped cream
Shredded coconut

Mix the sugar and egg yolks in top of a double boiler. Add the milk slowly, stirring constantly. Cook over boiling water until thickened, stirring frequently. Soften the gelatin in water. Add to milk mixture and stir until dissolved. Cool. Crumble the macaroons and stir into gelatin mixture. Beat egg whites with sherry until stiff and fold into gelatin mixture. Pour into a mold and chill for 4 hours. Turn out of mold, frost with whipped cream and sprinkle with coconut. 8 servings.

Mrs. Larry Luttrell, Mobile, Alabama

AROMATIC FIG PUDDING

2 1-lb. 1-oz. cans Kadota figs
2 env. unflavored gelatin
2 c. sour cream
Grated rind of 1 lge. lemon

Juice of 1 lge. lemon
2 tsp. angostura aromatic bitters
1/2 c. finely chopped nuts
3 eggs, separated

Drain the figs and reserve 1 1/2 cups juice. Cut the figs in quarters. Soften the gelatin in reserved fig juice in a saucepan for 5 minutes, then stir over low heat until gelatin is dissolved. Mix the sour cream with figs, grated rind, lemon juice, bitters, nuts and egg yolks. Stir in gelatin mixture gradually and blend well. Cool to room temperature. Beat the egg whites until stiff and fold into fig mixture. Pour into a 2-quart mold and chill until firm. Dip into warm water quickly and unmold. Serve cold with additional whole canned figs, if desired.

FRUITED COFFEE CREAM

1/2 9-oz. package dehydrated mincemeat	2 c. miniature marshmallows
1/4 c. cold water	1 c. hot strong coffee
	1 c. heavy cream, whipped

Combine the mincemeat and water in a saucepan and simmer until all the water is absorbed, stirring constantly. Add marshmallows to hot coffee in a bowl and stir until melted. Chill until thickened. Fold mincemeat into whipped cream, then fold in marshmallow mixture. Spoon into parfait glasses and garnish each serving with additional whipped cream and a walnut half. 8 servings.

Rev. Raymond G. J. Decker, Olney, Maryland

FILBERT MOUSSE

2 env. unflavored gelatin	2 tbsp. cognac (opt.)
1/3 c. water	1 tsp. vanilla
2 1/4 c. milk	1 1/2 c. ground toasted filberts
6 eggs, separated	1 c. heavy cream, whipped
1 c. sugar	Chopped toasted filberts

Soften the gelatin in water. Heat the milk in a heavy saucepan and stir in the gelatin until dissolved. Beat the egg yolks and sugar until light and fluffy and stir into hot milk gradually. Cook over low heat, stirring constantly, until mixture coats a spoon, but do not boil. Remove from heat and stir in cognac, vanilla and ground filberts. Chill until partially set. Beat egg whites until stiff, but not dry, and fold into filbert mixture. Fold in whipped cream and pour into a 5-cup souffle dish with 4-inch collar of waxed paper tied around outside top. Chill until set. Remove collar and garnish sides of mousse with chopped filberts. Yield: 8 servings.

LEMON-COCONUT CREAM DESSERT

2 1/2 c. half and half	3 eggs, separated
1 c. milk	1/2 lb. marshmallows
5/8 c. sugar	1/4 c. lemon juice
1/2 tsp. salt	1 tsp. lemon flavoring
1 env. unflavored gelatin	1 1/2 c. flaked coconut
1/2 c. cold water	3 c. vanilla wafer crumbs

Combine the half and half, milk, 1/4 cup sugar and salt in top of a double boiler. Cook over boiling water until scalded, stirring constantly. Soften the gelatin in cold water. Add to the milk mixture and stir until dissolved. Beat the egg yolks in a bowl until light. Stir in a small amount of milk mixture, then stir back into milk mixture. Cook until mixture coats spoon. Add marshmallows and stir until dissolved. Remove from heat and add the lemon juice and lemon flavoring. Chill until thickened. Beat egg whites until frothy. Add remaining sugar slowly and beat until stiff. Fold into gelatin mixture and fold in coconut. Place 2 1/2 cups wafer crumbs in a greased 13 x 9 x 2-inch pan. Place gelatin mixture on crumbs and sprinkle with remaining crumbs. Chill for 2 hours or overnight. Cut in squares to serve.

Mrs. W. R. Kinney, Woodward, Oklahoma

CHILLED LEMON SOUFFLE

2 tbsp. unflavored gelatin	1/4 c. sugar
1/2 c. lemon juice	Grated rind of 1 lemon
4 eggs	1 c. heavy cream, whipped
3 egg yolks	

Soften the gelatin in lemon juice and dissolve over hot water. Beat the eggs, egg yolks and sugar in a bowl until thick, then add gelatin mixture gradually. Fold in lemon rind and whipped cream. Tie a 6-inch band of waxed paper around a 1-quart casserole to form standing collar and fill casserole with lemon mixture. Chill until firm. 6-8 servings.

Mrs. H. H. Tippins, Griffin, Georgia

SUNNY SILVER LEMON DESSERT

3/4 c. melted shortening	1 c. cold water
Sugar	8 eggs, separated
1 c. sifted flour	Juice of 2 lemons
2 tbsp. unflavored gelatin	

Mix the shortening, 1 tablespoon sugar and flour and spread in a springform pan. Bake at 350 degrees until golden brown. Mix the gelatin and water and set aside. Beat the egg yolks in top of a double boiler until light. Add 1 cup sugar and lemon juice and mix well. Cook over boiling water until thick. Stir in gelatin mixture and cool. Beat egg whites until stiff, adding 1 cup sugar gradually. Fold into lemon mixture and pour into crust. Refrigerate overnight. Garnish with whipped cream and strawberry or cherry halves. 10 servings.

Mrs. Grady Evans, Crosbyton, Texas

CRANBERRY-RICE IMPERATRICE

1   14-oz. package precooked rice
1 qt. boiling water
2   3 1/4-oz. packages vanilla
    pudding and pie filling
1/3 c. sugar
3 c. milk
2 env. unflavored gelatin

1/4 c. cold water
1 tsp. vanilla
1 tsp. rum extract
2   2-oz. packages whipped
    topping mix
1   1-lb. can jellied cranberry
    sauce

Stir the rice into boiling water in a saucepan and remove from heat. Stir rice once, cover and cool to room temperature. Mix the vanilla pudding with sugar and 3 cups milk and cook according to package directions. Soak the gelatin in cold water for 5 minutes. Add to hot pudding and stir until gelatin is dissolved. Cool, then stir in vanilla and rum extract. Combine the rice and pudding mixture and chill until slightly thickened. Prepare whipped topping mix according to package directions and fold into rice mixture. Cut the cranberry sauce into 1/2-inch cubes. Spoon alternating layers of rice mixture and cranberry sauce into a lightly oiled 2 1/2-quart mold and chill until firm. Dip mold into lukewarm water, tap to loosen and invert on serving platter. Garnish with whipped cream and candied pineapple slices.

RICE-MACAROON CREAM

2 tbsp. unflavored gelatin
2 eggs, slightly beaten
2/3 c. sugar
3 1/3 c. evaporated milk

3 c. cooked rice
2 tsp. almond flavoring
24 toasted crushed macaroons

Soften the gelatin in 1/4 cup cold water in a saucepan. Add the eggs, sugar and 1 1/2 cups milk and mix well. Bring to a boil and reduce heat. Simmer until mixture coats a spoon, stirring constantly. Remove from heat and stir in rice. Chill until slightly thickened. Fold in flavoring. Freeze remaining milk in a refrigerator tray until ice crystals form around edges of tray. Place in a bowl and whip until stiff. Fold into rice mixture. Place alternate layers of rice mixture and macaroons in a 6-cup mold and chill until firm. 6 servings.

Mrs. June W. Galford, Dunmore, West Virginia

PINK CLOVER RICE MOLD

1 sm. package cherry gelatin	1 c. heavy cream
1 c. hot water	1/4 c. sugar
1 9-oz. can crushed pineapple	1 1/2 c. cooked rice, chilled
1/2 tsp. salt	

Dissolve the gelatin in hot water in a saucepan. Drain pineapple and reserve syrup. Add reserved syrup and salt to gelatin and mix well. Chill until partially set. Whip the cream until stiff and stir in sugar. Whip the gelatin until frothy and fold in the pineapple and rice. Fold in whipped cream and pour into a 1 1/2-quart mold. Chill until firm.

Mrs. John R. Fricker, Jr., De Valls Bluff, Arkansas

MAPLE MOUSSE

2 pkg. unflavored gelatin	1 pt. cream, whipped
1/4 c. cold water	1 c. chopped nuts
1 c. milk	1/2 lb. vanilla wafers, crushed
1 c. maple syrup	

Mix the gelatin and water. Bring milk to a boil in a saucepan and add maple syrup. Stir in the gelatin and cool. Fold in the whipped cream and nuts. Place alternate layers of wafer crumbs and gelatin mixture in a serving dish and refrigerate until firm.

Mrs. Jerry O'Neil, Carmen, Oklahoma

MACADAMIA NUT-DATE SOUFFLE

12 filled chocolate cookies, crushed	2 c. miniature marshmallows
	1/2 c. chopped macadamia nuts
1 8-oz. package dates, chopped	Whipped cream
3/4 c. water	Shaved chocolate
1/2 tsp. salt	

Press cookie crumbs into a well-greased 8-inch square pan. Combine dates, water and salt in a saucepan and simmer for 3 minutes. Add the marshmallows and stir until dissolved. Cool. Add nuts and place over cookie crumbs in pan. Refrigerate for several hours or overnight. Top with whipped cream and sprinkle with chocolate. 9 servings.

Mrs. Robert J. Keehn, Arlington, Virginia

APPLE MARSHMALLOW COOLER

3 med. apples	1 tbsp. flour
1 sm. can crushed pineapple	1 tbsp. sugar
1 c. chopped pecans	1 tsp. vinegar
30 marshmallows, quartered	1 c. milk
1 c. heavy cream	1/4 tsp. salt

Peel the apples and chop fine. Place in a bowl and add pineapple and pecans. Mix the marshmallows and cream in a bowl and set aside. Mix the flour, sugar, vinegar, milk and salt in a saucepan. Cook over medium heat, stirring constantly until thickened, then cool. Add to apple mixture and fold in marshmallow mixture. Refrigerate overnight. 10-12 servings.

Mrs. Chester Anderson, Erie, Tennessee

BING CHERRY DESSERT

1 No. 303 can Bing cherries	2 sm. bottles cola beverage
1 sm. can crushed pineapple	1 c. chopped pecans
2 sm. packages black cherry gelatin	Sweetened whipped cream (opt.)

Drain the cherries and pineapple and reserve the juices. Add enough water to combined juices to make 2 cups liquid. Pour into a saucepan and heat to boiling point. Add the gelatin and stir until dissolved. Cool. Stir in the cola beverage and chill until thickened. Add cherries, pineapple and pecans and pour into a mold. Chill until firm and serve with whipped cream.

Mrs. F. J. McGee, Dallas, Texas

CHEESE-FRUIT DESSERT

1 sm. package orange gelatin	1 c. cottage cheese
1 c. boiling water	1 c. crushed pineapple
2 c. miniature marshmallows	2 med. bananas, mashed
1 sm. can mandarin oranges	1/2 pt. heavy cream, whipped
1 sm. package cream cheese	

Dissolve the gelatin in boiling water in a bowl. Add marshmallows and stir until dissolved. Add oranges and mix well. Soften the cream cheese and stir into gelatin mixture. Fold in cottage cheese, pineapple and bananas. Fold in whipped cream and chill for 3 hours.

Maysie Grass, Ashland, Kentucky

PINEAPPLE MANDARIN

1 tbsp. unflavored gelatin	1 c. pineapple chunks
1/4 c. cold water	1 c. mandarin orange sections
1 3/4 c. pineapple juice	1 c. whipped cream
Yellow food coloring	6 maraschino cherries

Soften gelatin in cold water. Pour 1 cup pineapple juice into a saucepan and bring to a boil. Add gelatin and stir until dissolved. Add remaining pineapple juice and mix well. Add several drops of food coloring and chill until partially set. Spoon into 6 dessert dishes. Place 1/6 of the pineapple chunks and orange sections in each dish and chill until set. Top with whipped cream and cherries and serve.

Mrs. Lillian Herman, Bay City, Texas

MARASCHINO BAVARIAN CREAM

1 8-oz. jar red maraschino cherries	2 drops of red food coloring (opt.)
1 env. unflavored gelatin	2 tsp. vanilla
4 egg yolks	1 1/2 c. heavy cream
Sugar	Stemmed red maraschino
1/4 tsp. salt	cherries (opt.)
2 c. scalded milk	

Drain the cherries, reserving 1/4 cup syrup. Chop the cherries coarsely and drain on paper towels. Soften the gelatin in reserved syrup. Beat the egg yolks in a saucepan until foamy. Add 1/2 cup sugar and the salt, then blend in milk slowly. Cook over low heat, stirring constantly, until mixture comes to a boil. Remove from heat and stir in food coloring, gelatin mixture and 1 1/2 teaspoons vanilla until gelatin is dissolved. Cool, then chill until mixture mounds slightly when dropped from a spoon. Whip 1 cup heavy cream until soft peaks form. Beat gelatin mixture until fluffy and fold in whipped cream and chopped cherries. Pour into an oiled 1-quart mold and chill for 4 hours or until set. Unmold onto serving plate. Whip the remaining cream with 1 tablespoon sugar and remaining vanilla until soft peaks form. Pipe cream in center of mold and garnish with stemmed cherries. 8 servings.

LUSCIOUS DESSERT

1 No. 2 1/2 can fruit cocktail	1/2 c. mayonnaise or salad
1 sm. package lemon gelatin	dressing
1 c. hot water	1/4 c. quartered maraschino cherries
1/4 c. maraschino cherry syrup	1 1/2 c. miniature marshmallows
2 tbsp. lemon juice	1 c. heavy cream, whipped
2 3-oz. packages cream cheese	Red food coloring

Drain the fruit cocktail, reserving 1 cup syrup. Dissolve the gelatin in hot water in a bowl and stir in reserved syrup, cherry syrup and lemon juice. Chill until partially set. Soften the cream cheese. Add the mayonnaise and beat until smooth. Mix with gelatin mixture. Stir in fruits and marshmallows, then fold in whipped cream. Tint pink with food coloring and turn into a mold. Refrigerate for several hours. 18 servings.

Mrs. F. E. Rohling, Birmingham, Alabama

CHARLOTTE RUSSE

2 eggs, separated	1 c. heavy cream
2 tbsp. sugar	3 tbsp. powdered sugar
1/4 tsp. salt	1 tsp. vanilla
1 1/2 c. scalded milk	Light corn syrup
1 env. unflavored gelatin	1 1/2 to 2 doz. ladyfingers, split
1/4 c. cold water	

Mix the egg yolks, sugar and salt in top of a double boiler and add milk gradually. Cook over boiling water, stirring, until thickened. Soften the gelatin in cold water. Add to hot custard and stir until dissolved. Cool. Fold in stiffly beaten egg whites. Whip the cream with powdered sugar and vanilla until stiff and fold into custard mixture. Coat a baking dish with corn syrup and line with ladyfingers. Pour in custard mixture and refrigerate until chilled. Cut into squares. Top with additional whipped cream and cherries, if desired. One tablespoon sherry may be substituted for vanilla. 10-12 servings.

Mrs. Buford Williamson, Stoneville, Mississippi

FRESH STRAWBERRY RUSSE

2 env. unflavored gelatin	1/4 c. lemon juice
1/2 c. cold water	1 1/2 tsp. vanilla
3/4 c. hot water	1 3/4 c. crushed fresh
1/4 tsp. salt	strawberries
3/4 c. sugar	3/4 c. heavy cream, whipped

Soften the gelatin in cold water in a bowl. Add the hot water, salt and sugar and stir until dissolved. Add lemon juice, vanilla and strawberries and chill until thickened. Fold in whipped cream and chill until firm.

Mrs. Lois L. Brown, Oneonta, Alabama

MANDARIN AMBROSIA

2 tbsp. butter, softened	2 c. apricot juice
2 c. flaked coconut	1 6-oz. package lemon gelatin
1 11-oz. can mandarin oranges	1/2 c. heavy cream, whipped

Spread butter over bottom and side of an 8-inch round cake pan and press coconut into butter. Bake at 450 degrees for 15 to 20 minutes or until coconut is toasted. Cool. Drain the oranges and reserve juice. Mix the reserved juice with apricot juice and add enough water to make 3 cups liquid. Pour into a saucepan and bring to a boil. Add gelatin and stir until dissolved. Chill until syrupy and fold in oranges, reserving several segments for garnish. Spoon into coconut shell and chill until firm. Garnish with whipped cream and reserved orange segments. 6 servings.

Mrs. Anna Ruth Cheek, Taylorsville, Kentucky

PASHKA

1 1/2 c. cottage cheese	1/2 c. chopped blanched almonds
1/2 c. unsalted margarine	1/2 c. seedless raisins
1 3-oz. package cream cheese	1/2 c. mixed candied fruit
1/2 c. sugar	1/2 tsp. vanilla

Wash the cottage cheese and drain well to remove excess moisture. Cream the margarine in a bowl until fluffy. Add the cottage cheese and cream cheese and beat until smooth. Press through a strainer and stir in remaining ingredients. Line a large strainer with a clean cloth and turn the cheese mixture into strainer. Place a saucer, then a weight, such as a 1-pound box of salt, on top and let drain for 6 hours. Pack cheese mixture into 6 greased custard cups or individual molds and chill. Unmold and garnish with candied fruit.

PEACH MOUSSE

1 env. unflavored gelatin	1 c. sugar
1/4 c. cold water	1 c. mashed peaches
2 tbsp. lemon juice	2 c. cream, whipped

Soften the gelatin in the cold water and dissolve over boiling water. Place in a bowl and stir in the lemon juice, sugar and peaches. Chill until thickened. Fold in the whipped cream and chill until firm. 6 servings.

Mrs. G. M. Hall, Atlanta, Georgia

PEACHY PARFAITS

1 env. unflavored gelatin	Artificial sweetener equivalent
1/4 c. cold water	to 1/2 c. sugar
1 1/4 c. buttermilk	Yellow food coloring
1 tbsp. lemon juice	3 peaches, sliced
3/4 tsp. almond extract	

Soften the gelatin in cold water in a saucepan. Place over low heat and stir until gelatin is dissolved. Remove from heat and add the buttermilk, lemon juice, sweetener, almond extract and several drops of food coloring. Chill until mixture is consistency of unbeaten egg whites. Layer the gelatin mixture and peaches in 3 tall glasses, using about 2/3 cup gelatin mixture in each glass, and chill until firm. 3 servings.

Photograph for this recipe on page 1.

PEACH MAHARANI

1/2 lb. marshmallows, quartered	1/2 c. chopped pecans
1/2 c. orange juice	Sliced sponge cake
1/2 c. ginger ale	8 peaches, peeled and sliced
1 c. heavy cream, whipped	

Combine the marshmallows and orange juice in top of a double boiler and place over hot water. Stir until marshmallows are melted. Cool slightly and add ginger ale. Chill until thickened, then fold in whipped cream and pecans. Line a spring-form pan with waxed paper and place a layer of cake over waxed paper. Add half the peaches. Add half the marshmallow mixture and repeat layers. Chill overnight.

Mrs. C. A. Ashley, Ft. Lauderdale, Florida

POIRE GELEE EN CREME

1 15-oz. can Bartlett pears	1 3-oz. package cream cheese
1 sm. package orange gelatin	1/2 pt. whipping cream

Drain the pears and reserve juice. Pour reserved juice into a saucepan and bring to a boil. Add the gelatin and stir until dissolved. Refrigerate until partially set.

Soften the cream cheese. Blend the pears and cream cheese in a blender until smooth. Add the cream and gelatin mixture and blend well. Pour into a mold and chill until firm.

Mrs. Marion McBroom, Murfreesboro, Tennessee

FRESH PEARS IN WINE SYRUP

4 firm fresh pears	1/4 tsp. cinnamon
1 c. sugar	1/2 c. red Burgundy
2/3 c. water	2 c. sweetened whipped cream

Peel and core the pears. Combine the sugar and water in a saucepan and bring to a boil, stirring frequently. Reduce heat and stir in the cinnamon. Add the pears and simmer for about 10 minutes. Add the Burgundy and simmer for 5 minutes longer. Remove the pears to a dessert bowl and simmer liquid until syrupy. Pour over the pears and chill. Serve with whipped cream. 4 servings.

Mrs. Florence Joiner, San Antonio, Texas

CHARLOTTE A L'ORANGE

1 env. unflavored gelatin	1 6-oz. can frozen concentrated
2/3 c. sugar	orange juice
1/8 tsp. salt	1 c. evaporated milk
1/2 c. water	1 9-in. ladyfinger shell

Mix the gelatin, sugar and salt in a saucepan and stir in the water. Cook over low heat, stirring constantly, until gelatin and sugar are dissolved. Remove from heat and blend in orange juice concentrate. Chill until mixture mounds slightly when dropped from a spoon. Pour evaporated milk into freezer tray of refrigerator and freeze until ice crystals form around edges. Turn into a chilled bowl and whip with electric mixer at high speed until stiff. Fold in gelatin mixture and turn into ladyfinger shell. Chill until firm. Garnish with fresh orange sections.

fresh fruit

Fresh fruit . . . the dessert for all seasons. Yes, the endless changing of the seasons brings a never-ending variety of fresh fruit to your table. In the midst of winter, the family cheers ambrosia, that all-time southern favorite combination of coconut and citrus fruits. Spring signals the arrival of strawberry shortcake — the sweet mixture of ripe berries, soft cake, and fresh cream. As spring turns into summer, attention turns to melons — red, ripe watermelon, sweet cantaloup, and pale, delicious honeydew. Autumn means apples — at least half a dozen varieties, each with its own unique flavor — in cobblers, brown betties, dumplings.

With all this variety, smart southern homemakers have found that fresh fruit is just right on every occasion. For that all-important formal dinner, nothing surpasses the simple elegance of pears and cheese. And on a cold rainy winter night, cap your meal with fruit cobbler — made with one of the favorite recipes you'll find in the pages that follow. Just the sight and smell of any one of these dishes will warm every member of your family.

Fruit carries its own bonus for you, too. It not only is a great way to balance your budget, but it also balances your family's diet. In fact, for nutrition, attractiveness, economy, taste . . . fruit is nature's most perfect dessert!

The harvest's bounty — fresh fruit! And a boon to thrifty homemakers, too! Yes, fruits in all their brightly-colored glory lend a wide variety of flavors to the world of desserts. From a simple serving of fresh fruit with appropriate cheeses to elaborate fruit combinations baked to perfection — fruits add their own dimension to dessert making.

With the many fruits available almost year-round, fruit deserves a central place in the range of desserts. Buy in season — not only are prices lower but the quality of fruit is better. If a store advertises extraordinarily low-priced fruit, check it carefully. It may be bruised or pitted — suitable for canning and for some fruit desserts like cobblers.

Be sure to buy only ripe or nearly ripe fruit. Ripe pieces should be stored in the fruit and vegetable storage compartment of your refrigerator; unripened

FOR FRUIT DESSERTS

fruit should be stored in a cool, dark place and checked twice a day. As soon as it ripens, remove it to the fruit compartment.

FRESH FRUIT

Fresh fruit can be served in a variety of eye-pleasing ways. Melons, for example, such as Cantaloup, Honeydew, Casaba, and Watermelon are favorite taste treats. All should be served icy-cold. They may be served on a bed of cracked ice, but be sure that the ice touches only the rind. It may discolor the fruit pulp. For a gay treat, hollow out a watermelon half and use the pulp to form melon balls. Add balls from other melons, and you'll have a colorful and light dessert treat.

And don't forget the many berries available in local markets. Berries are a good buy, especially in summer. They should be unwrapped as soon as you arrive home, and spread in a single layer on a board or waxed paper. Pick them over carefully, removing the bruised or decayed pieces. Then gently wash the remaining berries and store them in the refrigerator. One of the most enjoyable — and easiest — of all desserts is nothing more than fresh strawberries dipped in confectionary sugar.

Try combining chunks of fresh, canned, and frozen fruit with their juices in a compote. A huge brandy snifter makes a lovely compote — and serves double-duty as an elegant and creative centerpiece! At dessert time simply dish the fruit into small individual snifters and serve.

If the flavor of your fruit is a bit too mild, marinate it in the juice of another fruit. You'll gain interesting taste combinations with grapes marinated in apple juice, apples in lemon juice, pineapple chunks in orange juice.

Fruits go well with certain liquers, too. In fact, a quick and elegant dessert is a mixture of fresh fruit chunks and a dash of dessert liquer — such as kirsch, cherry brandy, or cognac. If you prefer one of the lighter liquors, try adding a dash of rum or bourbon — the simplest fruits become extra-special flavor treats. When you want a fruit dessert appealing to the eye as well as to the palate, combine fresh apricot chunks and fresh strawberries with just a pinch of sugar, to bring out their natural juices. Before serving, lace with kirsch or brandy — a simple yet out-of-this-world dessert!

Another pleasant flavor combination is cheese and fruit — especially melons, grapes, pears, cherries, apples, or plums. Pears-with-cheese is an almost-classic dessert. Some cheeses that are particularly good with pears include Camembert, Roquefort, and Taleggio. These cheeses are excellent with other fruits, too. If your preference is for a milder cheese, try one of the great American cream cheeses. For variety, try serving some other cheeses to complement your fruit desserts — Gorgonzola, Brie, Gruyere, Liederkranz, or any other of the so-called "soft cheeses."

COOKED FRUIT

Fresh fruit is delicious just as it is, cooked and served with a light custard sauce, or as a topping for ice cream. It loses its flavor if soaked in water before it is cooked. Just pare, peel, and cut into cooking-sized pieces. (Always cut fruit with a stainless knife or its pulp will turn brown.)

The loss of natural sugars and vitamins, which sometimes occurs when fruit is cooked, can be minimized by using as little water as possible and cooking the fruit very briefly. Fresh fruit may be poached, pureed, baked, broiled, sauteed, or pickled. Please note: It is poached, never boiled. To poach fruit, drop it into boiling liquid, reduce the heat, and simmer until it is barely tender. Drain immediately to avoid mushiness. Soft, juicy fruits such as peaches should be poached in heavy sugar syrup that is boiling. As the end of the cooking time nears, plunge the pan into a pan of ice water to end the cooking process. Apples and similar hard fruits should be poached in water.

DRIED FRUIT

Modern dried fruits are delicious eaten right from the bag or they may be cooked. With modern food processing methods, it is no longer necessary to soak dried fruit before cooking. Rinse it thoroughly, place in a pan, fill with water to cover, and boil until very tender. Apples and apricots cook in about 40 minutes; figs in about 20, peaches in 50, pears in 40, prunes in 45 to 50, and raisins in 10. During the last five minutes of cooking time, add sugar to taste. If you are cooking figs, add sugar during the last 15 minutes of cooking time. For delicious added flavor, try adding stick cinnamon, cloves, or citrus fruit peel and juice to your cooking water.

Like cooked fresh fruit, dried fruits are delicious served by themselves, with sauces, or as an accompaniment to other desserts.

STRAWBERRY SHORTCAKE

2 c. flour	2/3 c. milk
1 1/2 tsp. baking powder	1 tsp. vanilla
1/2 tsp. salt	Butter
1 3/4 c. sugar	1 qt. strawberries
5 tbsp. shortening	

Preheat oven to 425 degrees. Sift the flour, baking powder, salt and 3/4 cup sugar together into a bowl and cut in shortening. Combine the milk and vanilla. Add to dry ingredients and mix well. Knead on a floured surface, then pat into a 10-inch round cake pan. Bake for about 15 minutes. Remove from pan and split. Butter while hot. Mash the strawberries and stir in remaining sugar. Place half the strawberries between shortcake layers and place remaining strawberries on top. Serve with whipped cream.

Mrs. Forest Babbs, Sturgis, Kentucky

STRAWBERRY-BANANA DESSERT

1 c. sugar	Juice of 1 lemon
1 qt. strawberries	1/2 c. toasted slivered almonds
2 tbsp. cornstarch	Cream
3 bananas, sliced thin	

Mix 1 cup sugar and 1 cup water in a saucepan and bring to a boil. Add the strawberries and cook over low heat until strawberries are soft but still whole. Blend cornstarch with small amount of cold water and stir into strawberry mixture. Simmer, stirring, for 3 minutes. Add bananas and lemon juice and pour into a serving dish. Cool. Sprinkle with almonds and serve with cream. 6 servings.

Mrs. Edna J. Griste, Sardis, Mississippi

STRAWBERRY COUER A LA CREME

1 lb. cottage cheese	1 c. heavy cream
1 lb. cream cheese, softened	Strawberries
4 tbsp. honey	

Drain the cottage cheese until dry. Mix the cream cheese and honey in a bowl. Add the cottage cheese and place in blender container. Blend until smooth. Pack into 4-cup mold. Place cheesecloth over top of mold and tie in place. Turn mold, cloth side down, over a plate and drain overnight or longer. Cut in wedges and serve with strawberries.

Mrs. W. M. Shearer, Springfield, Tennessee

STRAWBERRY STACK CAKE

1 pkg. refrigerator biscuits	Sweetened strawberries
Cooking oil	Whipped cream

Roll the biscuits separately on a floured surface until thin and pierce each several times with a fork. Fry in small amount of oil until brown and crisp, turning once. Cool. Place 1 biscuit on a platter and cover with strawberries. Repeat layers until all the biscuits are used, ending with strawberries. Serve with whipped cream.

Mrs. Alice Kinder, Tannersville, Virginia

FRUIT LUAU

1 can fruit cocktail, drained
Vanilla or strawberry ice cream
Pineapple rings

Whipped cream
1/2 c. strawberries or cherries

Place fruit cocktail in individual dessert dishes and add a layer of ice cream. Add a pineapple ring to each dish and fill centers with whipped cream. Top each serving with a strawberry.

Betty Williams, Lucedale, Mississippi

SYLLABUB

3 c. heavy cream
1/4 c. sugar

1/4 c. sweet sauterne
2 pt. fresh strawberries, sliced

Combine 2 cups cream, 2 tablespoons sugar and the sauterne in a large serving bowl and chill for 2 to 3 hours. Whip remaining cream with remaining sugar until soft peaks form. Top the sauterne mixture with strawberries, then with whipped cream. 8 servings.

APPLE WHIP

12 lge. marshmallows, quartered	1 ripe banana, mashed
1 c. orange or grape juice	1 c. heavy cream, whipped
1 lge. apple, grated	1/4 c. sugar

Place the marshmallows in orange juice in a bowl and let set until marshmallows are soft. Add the apple and banana and whip until fluffy. Fold in whipped cream and sugar and chill. Garnish with nuts. 8 servings.

Mrs. Carol Sailors, Tuscaloosa, Alabama

SPICED APPLES GLACE

6 lge. apples	6 maraschino cherries
2 c. sugar	2 tsp. cornstarch
3 c. water	1/4 c. cold water
6 thin lemon slices	Red food coloring
1 1-in. cinnamon stick	

Peel and halve apples and remove cores. Combine sugar and water in a large saucepan and bring to a boil. Add lemon slices, cinnamon and apples. Simmer for 15 minutes or until apples are tender but firm, then remove apple halves and lemon slices to a serving dish and garnish with cherries. Bring syrup in saucepan to a boil and cook until thick. Mix the cornstarch and cold water and stir into syrup. Cook for 2 minutes longer. Add several drops of food coloring and pour over apples. 6 servings.

Mrs. R. H. Winkler, Lenoir, North Carolina

APPLE CREAM

6 tbsp. flour	1 pt. milk
5/8 c. sugar	6 med. apples
Nutmeg to taste	

Mix the flour, sugar and nutmeg in a saucepan. Add a small amount of milk and stir until smooth. Add remaining milk and cook over low heat, stirring, until thickened. Peel the apples, cut in half and remove cores. Slice the apples and place in a baking dish. Pour milk mixture over apples. Bake at 325 degrees for 1 hour.

Mrs. W. James Crews, Summertown, Tennessee

DEEP-DISH APPLE DESSERT

1 qt. peeled sliced apples	1/4 tsp. salt
2/3 c. light corn syrup	1/2 c. soft margarine
1/2 c. sugar	1 c. flour

Place half the apples in a greased baking dish and pour corn syrup over apples. Add remaining apples. Mix remaining ingredients and press firmly over apples. Bake at 375 degrees for 1 hour or until apples are tender. Desired spices to taste may be added with apples.

Mrs. Myra B. Brown, Dawson, Georgia

BOSTON APPLES

5 lb. apples, cored and sliced	2 tbsp. lemon juice
1 c. (packed) brown sugar	Nutmeg to taste
1 c. apple cider	

Place the apples in a bean pot. Heat the sugar and cider in a saucepan until sugar is dissolved and remove from heat. Add lemon juice and nutmeg and pour over apples. Bake at 350 degrees for 1 hour.

Edwin Foster, Jr., Bradenton, Florida

MARIAN'S MISSOURI SHORTCAKE

4 pt. fresh strawberries, sliced	1 1/2 tsp. salt
Sugar	1 1/4 c. shortening
1/4 c. lemon juice	6 tbsp. water
3 1/3 c. sifted flour	1 1/2 c. heavy cream

Combine the strawberries, 1 cup sugar and lemon juice in a bowl and chill for 1 hour. Combine the flour and salt in a bowl and cut in shortening with pastry blender or 2 knives until mixture resembles coarse meal. Sprinkle with water and mix just until ingredients are blended. Press into a ball. Divide into 4 parts. Roll out each part on a lightly floured surface to 8-inch circle, trimming edges even with an 8-inch cake pan. Place circles on cookie sheets, sprinkle with sugar and prick with a fork. Bake in 425-degree oven for 15 minutes or until golden brown, then cool on racks. Drain strawberries and reserve syrup. Place 1 pastry circle on large serving plate and spoon 1/4 of the strawberries on pastry. Repeat layers with remaining pastry circles and strawberries. Whip the cream with 1 tablespoon sugar until stiff and mound on shortcake. Serve reserved syrup with shortcake. 10 servings.

BLUEBERRY ANGEL ROLL

1/3 c. sugar	1 15-oz. package angel food cake
1/4 c. cornstarch	mix
1 1/2 c. pineapple juice	Confectioners' sugar
1 12-oz. package frozen	
blueberries, thawed	

Mix the sugar and cornstarch in a saucepan and stir in the pineapple juice gradually. Cook over low heat, stirring constantly, until smooth and thick. Cool. Drain the blueberries and reserve syrup. Fold blueberries into pineapple sauce and chill. Prepare angel food cake according to package directions. Pour into an aluminum foil-lined and greased 10 x 15 x 1-inch baking pan. Bake in 375-degree oven for 12 to 15 minutes or until lightly browned. Sprinkle a towel with confectioners' sugar. Turn cake out of pan onto towel and remove the foil. Roll cake with towel as for jelly roll. Place on a cake rack until cool. Unroll cake and spread with blueberry filling. Remove towel. Reroll cake and place on a serving platter. Sprinkle with confectioners' sugar and chill. Spoon reserved blueberry syrup over roll and sprinkle lightly with confectioners' sugar. 6-8 servings.

Mrs. Nettie R. Burgess, Belton, South Carolina

MANGO BROWN BETTY

3 lge. mangos, sliced	1/4 c. (packed) brown sugar
1 c. malted cereal granules	1 tbsp. butter
Juice and grated rind of 1/2 lemon	1/2 c. water

Place half the mangos in a small baking dish and cover with 1/2 cup cereal granules. Add the lemon juice and grated rind. Add remaining mangos and add remaining cereal granules. Sprinkle with brown sugar and dot with butter. Add water. Bake at 375 degrees for 30 minutes. 6 servings.

Mrs. Annie S. Root, W. Palm Beach, Florida

WATERMELON DELIGHT

1/2 watermelon, chilled	3 lb. white grapes
3 cantaloupes, chilled	4 lb. fresh peaches, sliced

Remove seeds from watermelon and cantaloupes and scoop out pulp with melon scoop. Add the grapes and peaches and mix. Cut jagged edge around rim of watermelon half and place fruit mixture in watermelon. 12-15 servings.

Mrs. Gladys Jarrett, Hayesville, North Carolina

BLACKBERRY PUFF

1 c. butter	
1 1/8 c. sugar	4 egg whites, stiffly beaten
2 1/2 c. flour	1 c. heavy cream
3 1/2 tsp. baking powder	1/2 tsp. vanilla
1/2 c. milk	1 c. sweetened crushed blackberries

Cream the butter and 1 cup sugar in a bowl. Sift the flour and baking powder together and add to creamed mixture alternately with milk. Fold in the egg whites. Pour into well-greased custard cups and place in a roasting pan filled with 1 inch of hot water. Cover. Steam for 30 minutes and cool slightly. Remove from cups. Whip the cream in a bowl until stiff, adding remaining sugar and vanilla gradually. Fold in blackberries and serve over steamed mixture.

Mary S. Jackson, Columbus, Mississippi

CONTINENTAL FRUIT

1 1/2 c. sifted all-purpose flour	1 1-lb. 1-oz. can apricot halves
1/4 c. sugar	1 1-lb. can sliced peaches
1 tsp. grated lemon peel	1 1-lb. 4-oz. can sliced
3/4 c. butter or margarine	pineapple
1/2 c. oats	2 tsp. unflavored gelatin
2 egg yolks, slightly beaten	1 pt. fresh strawberries

Sift the flour and sugar together into a bowl. Add grated peel and cut in the butter until mixture resembles coarse crumbs. Stir in the oats. Add the egg yolks and stir lightly just until ingredients are mixed. Form into a ball and chill for at least 1 hour. Roll out 2/3 of the dough on a lightly floured board or canvas to form a 9-inch circle and place in a 9-inch springform pan. Press remaining dough about 1 3/4 inches up the sides of the pan. Prick bottom crust several times and chill for 10 minutes. Bake at 375 degrees for 25 to 30 minutes and cool thoroughly. Drain the canned fruits, reserving 3/4 cup liquid. Soften the gelatin in reserved liquid in a saucepan and heat over low heat, stirring constantly, until the gelatin is dissolved. Cool slightly. Brush the bottom crust with a thin coat of gelatin mixture with a pastry brush. Overlap canned fruits and strawberries in crust in layers, brushing fruits with the gelatin mixture as layered. Use all of the gelatin mixture. Chill until firm. 10-12 servings.

PEARS A LA MELBA

4 c. water
2 c. sugar
4 fresh pears with stems

1 pkg. frozen raspberries, thawed
1 qt. vanilla ice cream

Mix the water and sugar in a saucepan and bring to a boil. Add the pears and reduce heat. Simmer until the pears are tender but still whole. Remove pears from syrup, place on a dish and chill. Sieve the raspberries and add to syrup. Cook until thickened, then chill. Place the ice cream in 4 dessert dishes and place the pears on ice cream. Pour the raspberry syrup over pears and serve immediately.

Photograph for this recipe on page 150.

FRUIT COMPOTE

1 No. 2 1/2 can plums
1 No. 2 1/2 can whole apricots
1 No. 2 can pineapple spears
2 tbsp. lemon juice

3/4 tsp. nutmeg
1/4 c. honey
1 tbsp. salad oil

Drain the fruits and arrange in a large baking dish. Sprinkle with lemon juice and nutmeg and add honey and oil. Bake at 250 degrees until fruits are warm, basting occasionally with liquid in dish. Serve warm over ice cream balls or sponge cake.

Margaret W. Cyrus, Herndon, Virginia

REGAL FRUIT DESSERT

1 lge. can pineapple chunks
1 lge. can pear chunks
1 lge. bottle maraschino cherries
1/2 c. sugar
4 tbsp. flour

1 egg, beaten
4 red unpared apples
1 c. miniature marshmallows
1 c. chopped pecans

Drain the pineapple, pears and cherries and reserve pineapple and pear juices. Combine the sugar, flour, egg, reserved pineapple juice and 1/2 cup reserved pear juice in a saucepan and mix well. Cook over low heat until thick, stirring constantly, then cool. Remove cores from apples and cut apples into large pieces. Place in a bowl and add pineapple, pears, cherries, marshmallows and pecans. Pour sauce over top and chill for 24 hours.

Mrs. Hattie Pelfrey, Leeco, Kentucky

APPLE-DATE DESSERT

6 firm apples
18 pitted dates, chopped
Red food coloring (opt.)

2 lge. bananas, mashed
3 tsp. grated coconut

Remove cores from apples to within 1/4 inch of base. Mix dates with 1 drop of food coloring and stuff each apple with dates. Wrap each apple in square of aluminum foil with fluted top with 1 1/2-inch opening and place on cookie sheet. Bake at 350 degrees for 1 hour and 10 minutes. Open foil and top each apple with bananas and coconut, leaving foil open. Bake for 5 minutes longer.

Mrs. Charles W. Davis, Asheville, North Carolina

CURRIED FRUIT

1 No. 2 can peach halves	2 c. sliced apples (opt.)
1 No. 2 can pear halves	2/3 stick butter, melted
1 No. 2 can pineapple chunks	3/4 c. (packed) light brown sugar
1 sm. bottle maraschino cherries	2 to 4 tsp. curry powder

Drain the peaches, pears, pineapple and cherries and place in a 1 1/2-quart casserole. Add the apples and mix. Mix the butter, sugar and curry powder and spoon over fruits in casserole. Bake, covered, at 350 degrees for 1 hour. 6-8 servings.

Mrs. Thelma J. Haley, McRae, Georgia

FRUIT PARFAIT TORTONI

1 1-lb. 14-oz. can fruit cocktail	3 tbsp. brown sugar
1 bottle maraschino cherries	3/4 c. cookie crumbs
1 1/2 c. sour cream	1/2 c. toasted slivered almonds

Drain the fruit cocktail and cherries and cut the cherries in half. Mix the fruit cocktail and cherries. Combine the sour cream and brown sugar. Layer 1 tablespoon sour cream mixture, 2 teaspoons cookie crumbs, a sprinkle of almonds and 2 tablespoons fruit cocktail mixture in each of 6 parfait glasses. Repeat layers twice. Top with spoon of sour cream mixture and garnish with almonds. 6 servings.

Mrs. Annie R. Davis, Statesboro, Georgia

MILLIONAIRE DESSERT

2 eggs, beaten	1 can white cherries
5 tbsp. sugar	1 can pineapple chunks
5 tbsp. lemon juice	1/2 lb. colored marshmallows
2 tbsp. butter	1/4 lb. blanched almonds
1 c. heavy cream, whipped	

Combine the eggs, sugar and lemon juice in a double boiler and cook, beating constantly, until thick and smooth. Remove from heat and add butter. Cool, then fold in whipped cream. Cut the cherries into halves and add to whipped cream mixture. Add the pineapple, marshmallows and almonds and mix well. 8-10 servings.

Mrs. John Culbuson, Livingston, Tennessee

AMBROSIA

1 6-oz. can frozen orange juice	1 banana, mashed
1 8 1/2-oz. can crushed pineapple	1 7-oz. package grated coconut
3 apples, grated	

Thaw the orange juice and place in a bowl. Add the pineapple, apples, banana and coconut and mix well. Chill.

Mrs. Julia Whatley, Greenwood, South Carolina

FRUIT MACEDOINE

1 lge. can peach halves	1 lge. can applesauce
1 lge. can sliced pineapple	Butter
1 lge. can pear halves	Ginger to taste
1 lge. can apricot halves	

Drain the peaches, pineapple, pears and apricots and place in a large baking dish. Cover with applesauce and dot with butter. Sprinkle with ginger. Bake in 250-degree oven for 1 hour.

Mrs. Rudolph Small, Safford, Alabama

FRUIT LA FLEUR

1 can mandarin oranges	1 c. shredded coconut
1 lb. white grapes	1 c. sour cream
1 c. pineapple chunks	10 maraschino cherries
1 c. miniature marshmallows	

Drain the oranges and combine with remaining ingredients except cherries in a bowl. Garnish with cherries. Chill for several hours or overnight. 8-10 servings.

Mrs. Winne Rhodes, Wynona, Oklahoma

BAKED CERISE

1 can cherry pie filling	1 stick butter or margarine
1 pkg. white cake mix	Ice cream

Preheat oven to 375 degrees. Spread the pie filling in a 9-inch square baking pan and sprinkle with cake mix. Cut butter into thin slices and place over cake mix. Bake for 35 to 40 minutes. Cool and top with ice cream.

Mrs. Homer Kinder, Pikeville, Kentucky

FRENCH COBBLER

1/4 c. butter or margarine	1 tbsp. baking powder
1 c. flour	3/4 c. milk
1 3/4 c. sugar	1 can cherry pie filling

Melt the butter in a deep baking dish. Mix the flour, 1 cup sugar, baking powder and milk and pour into baking dish. Spoon pie filling over flour mixture and sprinkle remaining sugar over top. Bake for 20 to 25 minutes. Serve with whipped cream or ice cream, if desired. 6-8 servings.

Mrs. James M. King, Houston, Texas

CHERRY PIZZA DOLCE

2 c. prepared biscuit mix
2 tbsp. sugar
1/2 c. milk
3 tbsp. melted butter or
  margarine
1 1-lb. can apricot halves
1 tbsp. cornstarch
1/4 tsp. allspice
1/8 tsp. cinnamon
1 tsp. grated lemon peel

1/4 c. red maraschino cherry
  syrup
1/4 c. apricot jam
3 tbsp. cherry brandy (opt.)
1 c. red maraschino cherries
1/4 c. walnut halves
1/2 c. green maraschino cherries
1 8 3/4-oz. can pineapple
  tidbits, drained

Mix the biscuit mix and sugar in a bowl and stir in the milk and butter. Knead gently 10 times on lightly floured surface. Pat out on bottom and side of 12-inch pizza pan and prick with a fork. Bake in 450-degree oven for 10 to 15 minutes or until golden brown. Drain the apricots, reserving 1/2 cup syrup. Mix the cornstarch with spices and lemon peel in a saucepan and stir in the cherry syrup and reserved apricot syrup. Cook and stir until thickened and clear. Add the jam and stir over low heat until melted. Remove from heat and add brandy. Arrange circles of red cherries, walnuts, apricots and green cherries on pizza crust, beginning at outer edge. Fill center with pineapple tidbits and pour glaze evenly over all. Serve chilled or heated. Top each serving with a scoop of ice cream, if desired. 8 servings.

CHERRY CRUNCH

22 graham crackers, crushed	4 tbsp. flour
Sugar	1 can cherries
1 tsp. cinnamon	3 egg whites
1 stick margarine, melted	

Combine the cracker crumbs, 1/3 cup sugar, cinnamon and margarine in a bowl and mix well. Reserve 3/4 cup for topping and press remaining mixture on bottom and sides of 1 1/2-quart casserole. Mix the flour, cherries and sugar to taste in a saucepan and cook over low heat, stirring, until thickened. Pour into crumb-lined casserole. Beat the egg whites in a bowl until stiff, adding 6 tablespoons sugar gradually, and spread over cherry mixture. Sprinkle with reserved crumb mixture. Bake at 375 degrees for 35 minutes.

Mrs. Ivan Kessinger, Morgantown, Kentucky

UPSIDE-DOWN CERISE ROUGE

1 No. 2 can tart red cherries	Red food coloring
3/4 c. sugar	1 pkg. yellow cake mix
1 tbsp. butter	1/2 tbsp. cornstarch
1/4 tsp. almond flavoring	

Drain the cherries and reserve juice. Combine cherries, 1/2 cup sugar, butter, flavoring and several drops of food coloring in a saucepan and heat through. Pour into 8-inch round cake pan. Prepare cake mix according to package directions and pour over cherry mixture. Bake at 350 degrees for 35 to 40 minutes, then let stand for 10 minutes. Loosen side and invert onto serving dish. Add enough water to reserved cherry juice to make 1 cup liquid and pour into a saucepan. Stir in remaining sugar, cornstarch and 1/4 teaspoon food coloring and cook, stirring, until thickened. Serve with cherry pudding. 8-10 servings.

Mrs. Argo Carter, Sparta, Tennessee

ROYAL FARE

1 c. chopped dates	1 tbsp. flour
1 c. chopped pecans	1 tsp. baking powder
3/4 c. sugar	2 eggs, separated

Combine the dates, pecans, sugar, flour and baking powder in a bowl. Add the egg yolks and mix well. Fold in stiffly beaten egg whites and place in a greased casserole. Bake in 350-degree oven until brown.

Sauce

2 egg yolks	1 tbsp. brandy
3/4 c. sugar	1 c. whipped cream

Beat the eggs yolks well in a bowl. Add sugar and mix well. Add the brandy and cream and chill for at least 2 hours and 30 minutes. Serve over date mixture.

Mrs. C. A. Mayfield, Shreveport, Louisiana

PEACH MIETTE

4 c. sliced fresh peaches
1/2 c. (packed) brown sugar

3/4 c. graham cracker crumbs
Whipped cream or ice cream

Place the peaches in a shallow dish. Mix the sugar with crumbs and sprinkle over peaches. Toss lightly and chill. Top with whipped cream and serve.

Mrs. Danny Key, Morton, Texas

PEACHES NAPOLEON

6 peach halves
1/2 peeled grapefruit, sectioned

2 tbsp. honey
2 tbsp. brandy

Arrange peaches, cut side up, in a shallow dish. Fill hollows with grapefruit sections and drizzle honey over top. Bake in a 400-degree oven for about 15 minutes. Heat the brandy in a small pan and ignite. Pour over peaches and serve at once.

Mrs. Andrew J. Causey, Arlington, Texas

PEACH KUCHEN

2 c. sifted flour
1/4 tsp. baking powder
1/2 tsp. salt
7/8 c. sugar
1/2 c. butter

Sliced fresh peaches
1 tsp. cinnamon
2 egg yolks, beaten
1 c. sour cream

Preheat oven to 400 degrees. Combine the flour, baking powder, salt and 2 tablespoons sugar in a bowl. Cut in the butter until mixture is consistency of cornmeal. Press into 8-inch square pan. Cover with peaches and sprinkle with remaining sugar and cinnamon. Bake for 15 minutes. Mix the egg yolks and sour cream and pour over peaches. Bake for 30 minutes longer and serve hot or cold.

Mrs. R. C. Hatcher, Charleston, South Carolina

PEACH BROWN BETTY

1 can sliced peaches
3 c. stale bread crumbs
1/2 c. melted butter
1 c. (packed) light brown sugar

1/2 tsp. salt
1/2 tsp. cinnamon
Juice of 1/2 lemon

Place the peaches and bread crumbs in a bowl. Add the butter, sugar, salt, cinnamon and lemon juice and mix well. Pour into a greased casserole. Bake at 350 degrees until lightly browned. Serve with lemon sauce, whipped cream or ice cream.

Mrs. Clara Robinson, Morehead, Kentucky

PEACHES SUPREME

| 8 peach halves | 1/2 c. prepared mincemeat |
| 2 tbsp. melted butter | Sour cream |

Arrange the peach halves in a buttered baking dish and brush with melted butter. Place 1 teaspoon mincemeat in each half and spoon remaining mincemeat around peach halves. Bake at 350 degrees for 15 to 20 minutes or until peaches are lightly browned and top with sour cream. 8 servings.

FLAMING MINCEMEAT PEACHES

| 1 pkg. mincemeat | 1/4 c. brandy |
| 1 can peach halves, drained | |

Prepare mincemeat according to package directions. Place peach halves, cut side up, in oblong shallow casserole and fill each cavity with mincemeat. Broil for 5 to 10 minutes or until heated through. Heat the brandy in a saucepan and ignite. Pour over the peaches and serve.

Mrs. Victor Mandeville, Little Rock, Arkansas

BAKED GINGER PEACHES

| 1 No. 2 1/2 can peach halves | 1/2 tsp. ginger |
| 1/2 c. almond macaroon crumbs | 1 c. whipping cream, whipped |

Drain the peaches and reserve syrup. Place peaches in a greased shallow baking dish, cut side up. Mix crumbs and ginger with enough reserved peach syrup to moisten and fill peach centers with crumb mixture. Bake at 350 degrees for 15 minutes and serve hot or cold with whipped cream.

Mrs. Edgar Crenshaw, Channelview, Texas

CHOCOLATE PUDDING WITH PINEAPPLE

1 pkg. chocolate pudding mix	**Whipped cream**
1 No. 2 can crushed pineapple	**Grapes**

Prepare the pudding mix according to package directions. Fill parfait glasses 1/2 full with pudding and place in leaning position in refrigerator until set. Drain the pineapple and chill. Fill the parfait glasses with pineapple. Add dollop of whipped cream to each glass and top with grapes.

Photograph for this recipe on page 150.

QUELI

1 coconut	**2 doz. ladyfingers, split**
1 sm. can crushed pineapple	**3 1/4 c. orange juice**
2 c. sugar	**Juice of 2 lemons**

Drain the milk from coconut and reserve. Grate the coconut. Combine the pineapple, sugar and reserved coconut milk in a saucepan and mix well. Bring to a boil and cook until slightly thickened. Cool. Place layers of ladyfingers, pineapple mixture and coconut in a deep casserole until all ingredients are used, ending with coconut. Mix the orange juice and lemon juice and pour over coconut. Refrigerate for 24 hours. Serve with whipped cream. 16 servings.

Mrs. L. H. Carter, Monroe, Louisiana

PINEAPPLE-APPLE BETTY

3 c. sliced apples	**1/2 tsp. cinnamon**
1/2 c. crushed pineapple	**1/4 tsp. salt**
1/4 c. sifted flour	**1/4 c. butter or margarine**
1/2 c. (packed) brown sugar	

Place alternate layers of apples and pineapple in a greased 1 1/2-quart casserole. Mix the flour, sugar, cinnamon and salt together in a bowl and cut in butter. Sprinkle over pineapple mixture. Bake at 375 degrees for 30 minutes. Serve with cream, if desired. 6 servings.

Mildred F. McGee, Shreveport, Louisiana

PINEAPPLE-COCONUT DESSERT

1 No. 2 can crushed pineapple	**1 box white or yellow cake mix**
1 c. shredded coconut	**1/4 lb. butter, melted**

Place the pineapple in a buttered 9-inch cake pan. Sprinkle coconut over pineapple. Spread cake mix evenly over coconut and pour butter over cake mix. Bake at 350 degrees for 20 to 25 minutes or until lightly browned. Serve with whipped cream.

Mrs. Bertha Leicht, Perryton, Texas

PINEAPPLE ICEBOX DESSERT

1 lb. vanilla wafers, crushed	3 c. crushed pineapple, drained
1 1-lb. box confectioners' sugar	1 pt. whipping cream, whipped
1/2 lb. butter	1 c. chopped pecans
4 eggs	

Line 8 x 12-inch baking pan with half the wafer crumbs. Cream the sugar and butter in a bowl and add eggs, one at a time, beating well after each addition. Spread over crumbs. Add the pineapple and spread whipped cream over pineapple. Sprinkle with pecans and top with remaining crumbs. Garnish with additional whipped cream and cherries. 18-20 servings.

Mrs. W. C. Perry, Hurtsboro, Alabama

MARSHMALLOW DELIGHT

30 lge. marshmallows	14 graham crackers, crushed
1 c. milk	1 c. crushed pineapple, drained
1/2 pt. whipping cream	

Melt the marshmallows in milk in a double boiler and cool. Whip the cream until stiff. Place half the cracker crumbs in a 9-inch square pan. Add pineapple to marshmallow mixture and fold in whipped cream. Spoon onto crumbs and sprinkle remaining crumbs on top. Chill.

Mrs. R. E. White, Starkville, Mississippi

RHUBARB CRISP

4 c. chopped rhubarb	3/4 c. flour
1 tsp. cinnamon	1 1/2 c. sugar
1/2 tsp. salt	1/3 c. butter

Place the rhubarb in 6 x 10-inch baking dish and sprinkle with cinnamon and salt. Mix the flour, sugar and butter and sprinkle over rhubarb. Bake at 350 degrees for about 40 minutes. Serve warm with whipped cream or cream. 6-8 servings.

Mrs. Calvin Dickinson, Colonial Beach, Virginia

LEMON FROMAGE

1 pkg. lemon pudding mix	6 sm. oranges
1 c. whipped cream	

Prepare the pudding mix according to package directions. Cool and fold in the whipped cream. Cut through the peel of each orange to orange pulp in 6 equal parts, cutting 3/4 of the way to bottom. Remove orange from rind, leaving rind whole, then cut orange rinds in petal shape. Fill each orange rind with pudding and place on a flat dish. Chill. Separate orange into sections and place orange sections on top of pudding. Garnish with slivered almonds, if desired.

Photograph for this recipe on page 150.

FRESH PLUM PANDOWDY

2 1/2 lb. fresh plums	2 tbsp. butter
1 1/4 c. sugar	1 c. sifted all-purpose flour
3 tbsp. quick-cooking tapioca	2 tsp. baking powder
3/4 tsp. salt	3 tbsp. shortening
1/2 tsp. cinnamon	1/3 c. milk

Preheat oven to 375 degrees. Slice the plums and place in a bowl. Add 1 cup sugar, tapioca, 1/4 teaspoon salt and cinnamon and mix well. Turn into 8 x 8 x 2-inch baking dish and dot with butter. Combine the flour, remaining sugar, baking powder and remaining salt in a bowl and cut in shortening until mixture resembles crumbs. Stir in milk and drop from tablespoon onto plum mixture. Bake for 50 minutes or until done.

Georgia H. Ward, Neva, Tennessee

SPICY FRESH TANGERINE COMPOTE

6 to 8 med. to lge. tangerines	1 c. water
1 c. (firmly packed) brown sugar	1/2 tsp. whole cloves
1/2 c. honey	Shredded coconut

Grate 2 teaspoons peel from tangerines and reserve. Remove peel from tangerines carefully leaving fruit intact. Rinse fruit in cold water and scrape off any excess white membrane gently with a small knife. Remove white core from center of tangerines carefully and spread sections apart slightly to resemble flower petals. Place close together on a flat-bottomed dish in a standing position. Combine the sugar, honey and 1/2 cup water in a small, heavy saucepan. Bring to a boil and cook for 10 minutes, stirring occasionally. Remove from heat and add remaining water, cloves and reserved grated peel. Pour over the tangerines and refrigerate for several hours or until thoroughly chilled, basting frequently with syrup. Remove tangerines from syrup and drain slightly before placing on serving plate. Garnish center of tangerines with shredded coconut.

sweet breads

Bread-making is a very special art. And transforming breads into delicious desserts — the art of making sweet breads — seems to bring out the creative cooking genius of every woman. It does in southern homemakers, as the marvelous recipes in this section show.

As a homemaker prepares her old-fashioned favorite bread recipe, something inside her wants to try out a new filling . . . a new topping . . . or to substitute this ingredient for that. In subsequent bakings, she refines these changes until she has a new favorite recipe, one uniquely her own. This recipe brings warm words of praise from family and friends — it becomes her specialty, the one dish for which she is best known. Recipes such as these are family treasures, handed down from one generation to another. This section is a treasury of such recipes. Muffins . . . biscuits . . . doughnuts . . . nut breads . . . rolled breads . . . these and many more sweet breads are represented.

Perhaps as you work with your bread dough, your creative imagination will be working, too. You will begin to substitute ingredients, to add your own touches. You will be enjoying that very special pleasure of bread-making — inventiveness! And adding to your pleasure are the compliments your creations bring from everyone who enjoys them. Try it today — you'll see!

Sweet breads are an imaginative way to crown a meal. Of all the sweet breads, coffee cakes are probably the most versatile and the best-loved. Every homemaker has her favorite coffee cake recipe — the one she serves on special occasions. Many such recipes are variations of traditional coffee cakes which have been developed in other lands — German Kugelhopf or French brioche, for example. Variations come in the combinations of spices used and in the shaping of the dough.

Recipes for traditional sweet breads are rich in eggs and butter. Sometimes sour cream is added to make them even richer. The finest sweet bread dough is made with egg yolks. If you have such a recipe, whole eggs can be substituted for yolks at the ratio of one whole egg for every two yolks.

Every homemaker knows the disappointment of having her coffee cake taste

cooking methods

FOR SWEET BREADS

flat. Many times, this problem can be easily overcome with a little imagination. Some expert bread makers recommend tinting the dough slightly yellow — the additional color gives the visual impression of a much richer dough. To perk up the flavor of your coffee cake, use crushed macaroons, almond paste, rolled cake crumbs, or finely ground nuts in the topping mixture. Nuts that go well with coffee cake include hazelnuts, pecans, walnuts, almonds, and brazil nuts. Avoid using coconut or peanuts unless specifically called for in your recipe.

Another good perker-upper is a small amount of lemon juice or grated lemon rind added to the dough itself. Dried currants or a bit of finely chopped citron, added before the final rising of the dough, will also bring out the full flavor of your coffee cake.

When filling your coffee cake, a 9-inch ring cake will take about a cup of filling; individual rolls take two teaspoons each. For an unusual taste treat, substitute your favorite marmalade for the filling the recipe calls for.

The sweet breads you make with yeast will last longer and reheat better than the so-called "quick breads," which should be served immediately following baking. Fruit and nut breads taste best if they are wrapped in foil after baking and chilled for 12 hours. This time allows the full richness of the fruit and nut flavors to ripen and blend.

Here are some tried-and-proven suggestions for extra-special sweet breads:

Handle the dough with care. Yeast breads can be thoroughly kneaded without problems. In preparing quick breads, mix the liquid with the dry ingredients only enough to dampen them. If kneading is specified, do it quickly and very lightly.

Use your family's favorite taste treats to highlight your dessert breads. For example, brush the tops of muffins or biscuits with melted butter and sprinkle with maple sugar. Bake and serve, and listen to the compliments. Or add blueberries, chopped dried fruit, nuts, or chopped cranberries-and-oranges to your muffin batter. Sprinkle the individual muffins with a pinch of sugar and bake. A delight to smell and a treat to eat!

Decorate your sweet breads with a thin icing in one of the fruit flavors. Top with pieces of candied fruit, and you've got a beautiful dessert that will be the highlight of any meal!

For an eye-pleasing treat, try baking your sweet breads in something other than the usual bread pans. For a ladies' luncheon or bridge party, bake your breads in 6-ounce juice cans. Fill the cans not more than 3/4 full. Slices of these miniature breads will be a perfect size for ladies.

FREEZING SWEET BREADS

One reason sweet breads are such popular desserts is that they are easily frozen. Bake two or three at a time and freeze those you don't use right away. Weeks later, when you're in a hurry or perhaps don't feel like cooking, pop it out of the freezer and, presto, your dessert is ready.

Most sweet breads freeze well. The yeast-type breads freeze better than the quick ones. Before freezing, let the bread cool thoroughly, preferably overnight. Wrap it with clear wrapping, then with aluminum foil or freezer wrap. Mark the contents and the date clearly on the package. Sweet breads keep in the freezer for up to six months.

When you're ready to use the frozen breads, you can thaw them in your oven. Preheat the oven to 300 degrees and place the wrapped bread in the oven for 30 minutes. One word of caution: if you have wrapped your bread in one of the plastic wraps, unwrap it, remove the plastic wrap, and rewrap in foil or freezer paper. If moisture forms on the bread during thawing, unwrap it and let stay in the oven an additional 5 minutes.

FRESHENING SWEET BREADS

If your sweet bread has become slightly stale in storage, it's easy to make it fresh again. Place it in a paper bag and seal the bag tightly. Sprinkle with water and place in 350-degree oven until the bag is dry. Serve at once.

Coffee cakes are just some of the delicious sweet breads you'll be making for your family with the recipes in this section. Apricot breads . . . biscuits . . . crepes . . . doughnuts . . . muffins . . . nut breads . . ., recipes for these and many more flavorful desserts abound. You're certain to find just the recipe you've been looking for to delight your family and guests.

SAVARIN CREME CHIBOUST

1/2 c. milk	2 1/2 c. sifted all-purpose flour
1/4 c. butter or margarine	3/4 c. toasted chopped filberts
1/2 c. sugar	1 8-oz. jar red glace cherries,
1/2 tsp. salt	chopped
1 pkg. dry yeast	Rum-Flavored Syrup
1/4 c. warm water	Apricot Glaze
2 eggs, beaten	12 glace cherries, halved
1/2 tsp. grated lemon peel	Creme Chiboust

Scald the milk in a saucepan and stir in the butter, sugar and salt. Cool to lukewarm. Sprinkle the yeast over warm water in a large bowl and stir until dissolved. Blend in milk mixture. Add the eggs, lemon peel and flour and beat vigorously for 5 minutes. Cover and let rise in a warm place for about 1 hour and 30 minutes or until almost doubled in bulk. Stir down and beat in filberts and chopped cherries. Turn into a well-greased 9-inch ring mold. Cover and let rise for about 1 hour or until doubled in bulk. Bake in 350-degree oven for 50 minutes and turn out onto deep platter. Pour hot Rum-Flavored Syrup over savarin slowly until all syrup is absorbed, then cool. Glaze ring with half the warm Apricot Glaze. Arrange cherry halves in design over glaze and spoon remaining glaze over cherries. Cool. Fill center of ring with Creme Chiboust. Garnish with whipped cream and 6 quartered glace cherries, if desired.

Rum-Flavored Syrup

1 c. water	1 long strip lemon peel
3/4 c. sugar	2 tsp. rum extract
1 long strip orange peel	

Mix the water, sugar, orange peel and lemon peel in a saucepan and bring to a boil. Remove from heat and stir in rum extract. Remove peels and discard.

Apricot Glaze

1/2 c. strained apricot preserves   **2 tbsp. sugar**

Combine the apricot preserves and sugar in a saucepan. Cook and stir over high heat for 2 to 3 minutes or until mixture coats a spoon with a light film.

Creme Chiboust

3 eggs, separated	**1/4 tsp. rum extract**
3/4 c. sugar	**1 env. unflavored gelatin**
1/4 c. flour	**1/4 c. water**
1 c. milk	**1 c. heavy cream**
1/2 tsp. vanilla	

Blend the egg yolks and 1/2 cup sugar in a bowl and mix in flour. Pour milk into a saucepan and bring to a boil. Stir in vanilla and rum extract, then add to sugar mixture gradually, stirring constantly. Return mixture to saucepan and bring to a boil, stirring constantly. Remove from heat. Soften gelatin in water and stir into hot mixture until dissolved. Stir in cream. Beat the egg whites in a bowl until stiff, adding remaining sugar gradually. Add cream mixture gradually, beating constantly, then chill for at least 1 hour and 30 minutes. Beat well just before serving.

APPLE LOAF

2/3 c. butter	**2 tsp. baking powder**
1 1/3 c. sugar	**1 tsp. soda**
4 eggs	**1 tsp. salt**
2 c. applesauce	**1 tbsp. grated lemon rind**
1/2 c. milk	**2/3 c. chopped candied cherries**
4 c. sifted flour	**1 1/2 c. chopped nuts**

Cream the butter and sugar in a bowl and beat in eggs, one at a time. Stir in applesauce and milk. Sift the flour, baking powder, soda and salt together. Add to creamed mixture and mix well. Add lemon rind, cherries and nuts and pour into 2 greased and floured loaf pans. Bake at 350 degrees for 1 hour.

Mrs. W. G. Harper, Bessemer, Alabama

FRUIT KOLACHE

1 pkg. dry yeast	**1/3 c. sugar**
1/2 c. warm water	**1 tbsp. salt**
1/4 c. butter or margarine	**4 to 5 c. flour**
1 c. scalded milk	**Cooked mashed apricots**
1 egg, beaten	

Dissolve the yeast in warm water. Melt the butter in milk in a bowl. Add the egg, sugar and salt and mix well. Add yeast. Add enough flour, small amount at a time, for stiff dough. Let rise until doubled in bulk, then punch down. Roll out on floured surface into 15-inch square and cut into 3-inch squares. Place 1 spoon apricots in each square and bring corners together. Place 2 inches apart on greased baking sheet and let rise until doubled in bulk. Bake at 400 degrees for 30 to 40 minutes.

Mrs. W. F. White, Fort Worth, Texas

APRICOT BREAD

1 c. chopped dried apricots	3 c. flour
1/4 c. boiling water	2 tsp. baking powder
1 c. sugar	1/2 tsp. soda
1 c. (packed) brown sugar	1/2 tsp. salt
2 eggs, beaten	1 c. chopped nuts
1 c. sour milk or buttermilk	

Place the apricots in boiling water and let set. Combine the sugars, eggs and sour milk in a large mixing bowl. Add the flour, baking powder, soda and salt and mix well. Drain the apricots and add to flour mixture. Stir in nuts and pour into 4 greased loaf pans. Bake in 350-degree oven for 10 minutes. Reduce temperature to 300 degrees and bake for 30 to 40 minutes longer. Remove from pans and cool on rack. Wrap in plastic wrap and store for 24 hours before slicing.

Helen S. Redmon, Greensboro, North Carolina

SPICY APRICOT BREAD

1 1/2 c. chopped dried apricots	1/4 tsp. nutmeg
1 c. water	1/2 tsp. salt
1 c. sugar	2 c. flour
6 tbsp. shortening	1 tsp. soda
1/2 tsp. cinnamon	1 egg, beaten
1/2 tsp. cloves	

Place the apricots in a saucepan with water, sugar, shortening, cinnamon, cloves, nutmeg and salt and bring to a boil. Cook over medium heat for 5 minutes, stirring occasionally, then cool. Place in a mixing bowl. Sift flour with soda. Stir egg into apricot mixture and stir in flour mixture until just blended. Pour into greased and floured loaf pan. Bake in 350-degree oven for 1 hour and cool for 5 minutes before removing from pan.

Estelle J. Garrison, Fayette, Alabama

BANANA-NUT BREAD

1/2 c. vegetable oil	1/2 tsp. baking powder
1 c. sugar	1/2 tsp. salt
2 beaten eggs	3 tbsp. milk
3 bananas, mashed	1/2 tsp. vanilla
2 c. sifted flour	1/2 c. chopped nuts
1 tsp. soda	

Beat the oil and sugar together in a bowl. Add eggs and bananas and beat well. Sift the flour, soda, baking powder and salt together and add to oil mixture alternately with milk and vanilla. Beat well and stir in nuts. Pour into 9 x 5-inch greased loaf pan. Bake at 350 degrees for about 1 hour. Cool and store in airtight container.

Mrs. Carrie Carey, Louisa, Kentucky

RUSSIAN HOLIDAY BREAD

2 pkg. yeast	1 c. raisins
1/2 c. sugar	1/2 c. slivered toasted almonds
2 tsp. salt	7 2/3 c. sifted all-purpose flour
2/3 c. instant nonfat dry milk	3 c. sifted powdered sugar
2 eggs	1 tsp. lemon juice
1/2 c. soft shortening	1 tsp. grated lemon rind
1/2 tsp. yellow food coloring	

Place the yeast in a 3-quart bowl. Add 1/2 cup lukewarm water and stir just until yeast is dissolved. Add the sugar, salt, dry milk, eggs, shortening, 1 1/2 cups water, food coloring, raisins and almonds and mix well. Stir in 1/2 of the flour. Add remaining flour and mix well. Turn onto lightly floured board and knead until smooth and elastic. Place in a greased bowl and turn to grease top. Cover with waxed paper, then with a towel. Let rise in a warm place for about 45 minutes or until doubled in bulk. Punch down and let rise again until almost doubled in bulk. Punch down and divide into 4 portions. Form into balls and place in 4 well-greased 1-pound coffee cans. Let rise until doubled in bulk and place cans on cookie sheet. Bake at 375 degrees for about 40 minutes or until well browned. Loosen around sides of cans with a knife and remove from cans. Place on wire rack. Mix the powdered sugar, 3 tablespoons water, lemon juice and lemon rind in a 1 1/2-quart bowl until blended. Drizzle over tops of loaves while still warm, allowing glaze to drip over the sides. Sprinkle with tiny colored decorettes.

Photograph for this recipe on page 170.

PUMPKIN BREAD

3 c. flour	1/2 c. chopped nuts
1 tsp. soda	4 eggs, beaten
1 tsp. salt	2 c. cooked mashed pumpkin
3 tsp. cinnamon	1 1/4 c. melted shortening
2 c. sugar	

Sift the dry ingredients into a large mixing bowl. Add the nuts and stir well. Form a well in center and add eggs, pumpkin and shortening. Stir until moistened. Pour into 2 well-greased loaf pans. Bake at 350 degrees for 45 to 50 minutes or until done.

Mrs. Virginia Crum, Ashland, Kentucky

STRAWBERRY DESSERT BREAD

3 c. flour	2 pkg. frozen strawberries,
1 tsp. soda	thawed
1 tsp. salt	4 eggs, well beaten
3 tsp. cinnamon	1 1/4 c. oil or melted shortening
2 c. sugar	1 1/4 c. chopped pecans

Sift dry ingredients together into a large bowl and make a well in the center. Mix remaining ingredients and pour into dry ingredients. Stir just enough to dampen all ingredients and pour into 2 greased loaf pans. Bake at 350 degrees for 1 hour.

Mrs. Lillian Herman, Bay City, Texas

SHREDDED WHEAT BREAD

3 shredded wheat biscuits	3 tbsp. shortening
2 1/4 c. lukewarm water	1/2 c. dark molasses
1 pkg. dry yeast	5 c. flour, sifted
2 tsp. salt	

Crumble shredded wheat biscuits into a bowl and add 2 cups water. Dissolve yeast in remaining water. Add yeast, salt, shortening and molasses to shredded wheat mixture and mix well. Add flour and mix thoroughly. Knead lightly on well-floured board. Place in a greased bowl and cover with a cloth. Let rise in a warm place for 2 hours. Divide into 2 parts and shape into 2 loaves. Place in bread pans and cover. Let rise in warm place for 2 hours. Bake at 350 degrees for 45 minutes.

Mrs. Frank V. Young, Columbia, Kentucky

MALTED CEREAL BREAD

1 c. malted cereal granules	3 3/4 c. sifted flour
2 c. sour milk	4 tsp. baking powder
1 egg	1 tsp. soda
3/4 c. sugar	1 1/2 tsp. salt
3 tbsp. melted shortening	

Combine the cereal and sour milk in a bowl and let stand for 15 minutes. Beat the egg and sugar together and add to cereal mixture. Add the shortening and mix well. Sift flour, baking powder, soda and salt together. Add to cereal mixture and beat until smooth. Turn into 2 greased 8 x 4 x 3-inch loaf pans and let stand for 45 minutes. Bake in 350-degree oven for 1 hour or until done.

Mrs. Ruth Schreier, Leesburg, Florida

LEMON BREAD

1/2 c. shortening	1 tbsp. baking powder
1 1/2 c. sugar	1 c. milk
2 eggs, slightly beaten	1 c. chopped nuts
1 2/3 c. sifted flour	Grated rind of 1 lemon
1/2 tbsp. salt	Juice of 1 lemon

Cream the shortening with 1 cup sugar in a large bowl, then add eggs. Sift flour with salt and baking powder and add to the creamed mixture alternately with milk. Mix in nuts and lemon rind and place in greased 5 x 9-inch pan. Bake at 350 degrees for 1 hour. Combine remaining sugar with lemon juice and pour over hot bread. Cool, then wrap in foil.

Mrs. Henry T. Washington, Dahlgren, Virginia

OATMEAL BREAD

2 pkg. yeast	2 c. boiling water
4 tbsp. lukewarm water	1 c. rolled oats

2 tbsp. melted butter

1 tsp. salt

3/4 c. (packed) brown sugar

1/2 c. finely chopped nuts

4 to 4 1/2 c. flour

Soften the yeast in lukewarm water. Pour boiling water over oats in a large bowl and let stand until lukewarm. Add the butter, yeast, salt, sugar and nuts and mix well. Add the flour and mix thoroughly. Knead on a floured surface until smooth and elastic. Cover and let rise until doubled in bulk. Knead well and place in 2 greased loaf pans. Let rise until doubled in bulk. Bake at 300 degrees for about 40 minutes or until done. Grease top with additional butter.

Mrs. Norrie S. Smylis, Enterprise, Mississippi

MEDITERRANEAN FEAST BREAD

1/4 c. warm water

1 pkg. dry yeast

1/2 c. milk, scalded

2 tbsp. softened butter or
  margarine

1/4 c. sugar

1 tsp. salt

1 egg, slightly beaten

3 1/2 to 3 3/4 c. sifted
  all-purpose flour

1/2 c. chopped red maraschino
  cherries

1 tbsp. grated lemon peel

Thin confectioners' sugar
  glaze (opt.)

Pour the warm water into a large bowl. Add the yeast and stir until dissolved. Cool the milk to lukewarm and stir into yeast. Stir in butter, sugar, salt and egg. Stir in half the flour, cherries and lemon peel and mix well. Add enough remaining flour gradually until dough can be handled easily. Knead on lightly floured board for 10 minutes or until smooth and elastic. Shape into a ball and place in oiled bowl. Cover with a towel and let rise in warm place for 1 hour and 30 minutes to 2 hours or until doubled in bulk. Punch down and shape into 3 round loaves. Place on a lightly greased baking sheet 1/2 inch apart to form 3-leaf clover. Cover with a towel and let rise until doubled in bulk. Bake in 350-degree oven for 30 to 35 minutes. Frost with glaze. Garnish each loaf with 3 red glace cherry halves to form flower and red glace cherry slice to form stem. Serve with butter.

UPSIDE-DOWN ORANGE-NUT BISCUITS

2 c. sifted flour	1/2 c. orange juice
1 tbsp. baking powder	2 tsp. grated orange rind
1/2 tsp. salt	1/4 c. shortening
1/2 tsp. cinnamon	3/4 c. milk
3/4 c. sugar	1/2 c. chopped nuts
1/4 c. butter or margarine	

Sift the flour, baking powder and salt together. Mix the cinnamon and 1/4 cup sugar. Combine the butter, orange juice, remaining sugar and orange rind in a saucepan and cook for 2 minutes. Pour into 12 medium muffin cups. Cut shortening into flour mixture and stir in milk. Knead on floured surface for 30 seconds. Roll out into a 12-inch square and sprinkle with cinnamon mixture and nuts. Roll as for jelly roll and cut into twelve 1-inch slices. Place, cut side down, over orange mixture in muffin cups. Bake at 450 degrees for 20 to 25 minutes.

Mrs. Richard Midkiff, Glenwood, West Virginia

PINEAPPLE TURNOVER BISCUITS

1 9-oz. can crushed pineapple	10 walnut halves
1/4 c. brown sugar	1 10-count pkg. refrigerator
2 tbsp. melted butter	biscuits
1/2 tsp. ground cinnamon	

Drain the pineapple and reserve syrup. Combine pineapple, brown sugar, butter and cinnamon and place in 10 greased muffin cups. Place 1 walnut half and 1 teaspoon reserved syrup in each cup and top with biscuits. Bake at 425 degrees for 12 to 15 minutes and cool for 1 minute before removing muffins from pan.

Mrs. Earnest Thomas, Jayton, Texas

PUMPKIN BISCUITS

3 c. flour	1 tbsp. shortening
3 tsp. baking powder	4 tbsp. brown sugar
1 tsp. salt	1 c. cooked mashed pumpkin

Mix the flour, baking powder and salt in a bowl and cut in shortening. Stir in sugar and pumpkin and mix well. Pat to 1-inch thickness on a floured board and cut with a biscuit cutter. Place on a greased baking sheet. Bake at 425 degrees for 20 minutes.

Mrs. Iona C. O'Brien, St. Petersburg, Florida

BLINTZES WITH STRAWBERRIES

5 eggs	2 c. strawberry preserves
1 c. flour	1 1/2 lb. dry cottage cheese
1 tsp. salt	1 tbsp. sugar
1 c. milk	Honey
Butter	Sour cream

Blend 4 eggs, flour, salt and milk in an electric blender. Heat a heavy 10 or 12-inch skillet and grease with butter. Pour in 1 cup batter and rotate skillet quickly so that thin layer covers bottom of skillet. Pour excess batter back into blender. Cook over medium-high heat till edges pull away from side of skillet, but do not turn. Turn out onto towel. Repeat till all batter is used, buttering pan and stirring batter as needed. Combine 1 cup preserves, cottage cheese, remaining egg, 1 tablespoon melted butter and sugar and place 1 spoon in center of unbaked side of each pancake. Fold into square envelope and fry in honey over low heat for 5 minutes on each side. Place 1 spoon sour cream on top of each square and place 1 spoon preserves on top of sour cream. Filling may be varied, if desired.

Mrs. D. M. Smith, Dallas, Texas

BLUEBERRY BAKE

1/3 c. scalded milk	1 egg, beaten
3/8 c. sugar	1 1/3 c. flour
1/2 tsp. salt	1 can blueberries, drained
6 tbsp. margarine	3 tbsp. brown sugar
1 pkg. dry yeast	1/2 tsp. cinnamon
1/4 c. warm water	Thin confectioners' sugar icing

Mix the milk, 1/4 cup sugar, salt and 3 tablespoons margarine in a bowl and cool to lukewarm. Dissolve the yeast in warm water and stir into milk mixture. Add egg and flour and beat until smooth. Spread in greased 9-inch square pan and sprinkle with blueberries. Mix the brown sugar, remaining sugar and cinnamon and sprinkle over blueberries. Dot with remaining margarine and cover. Let rise in warm place, free from drafts, for about 40 minutes or until doubled in bulk. Bake at 400 degrees for 25 minutes and drizzle with icing while warm.

Mrs. H. Robert Black, Austin, Texas

BRUNCH CAKE

1/2 c. margarine	1/4 c. milk
1 8-oz. package cream cheese	2 c. sifted flour
1 1/4 c. sugar	1 tsp. baking powder
2 eggs	1/2 tsp. soda
2 tsp. vanilla	1/4 tsp. salt

Mix the margarine and cream cheese in a bowl. Add the sugar gradually and cream well. Beat in eggs, one at a time. Add the vanilla and milk and mix well. Sift remaining ingredients together and stir into egg mixture. Pour into a greased and floured 9 x 13-inch pan.

Topping

1/3 c. (packed) brown sugar	1/2 tsp. cinnamon
1/3 c. flour	2 tbsp. margarine

Combine all ingredients and mix well. Sprinkle over batter. Bake in 350-degree oven for 35 to 40 minutes.

Mrs. Edwin Nehring, Austin, Texas

REBEL COFFEE RING

1 10-count pkg. refrigerator biscuits	1 tbsp. water
1/4 c. melted butter or margarine	10 candied cherries
1 c. finely chopped peanuts	1/2 lb. cheese
1/2 c. powdered sugar	

Separate the refrigerator biscuits. Dip both sides of the biscuits in melted butter, then dip both sides in the chopped peanuts, coating well. Arrange in an overlapping circle on a greased baking sheet. Bake in a 425-degree oven for 10 to 15 minutes or until the biscuits are brown. Mix the powdered sugar and the water in a bowl, then drizzle over the hot coffee ring. Place the candied cherries on the powdered sugar mixture between each biscuit. Slide the coffee ring onto a doily on a serving plate. Cut the cheese in cubes and place in center of the coffee ring. Serve warm. Additional peanuts may be sprinkled over the powdered sugar mixture, if desired. 6-8 servings.

BOWKNOTS

2 eggs	1/2 tsp. cream of tartar
1/3 c. sugar	1/4 tsp. salt
1 tbsp. cream	1/4 tsp. mace
1 tbsp. melted butter	1/8 tsp. soda
Flour	Powdered sugar

Beat the eggs in a bowl. Add the sugar, cream and butter and mix well. Sift 1 cup flour with cream of tartar, salt, mace and soda and stir into egg mixture. Stir in enough flour to make a stiff dough. Roll small pieces of dough into pencil-sized shapes and tie in single knots. Fry in deep, hot fat until brown and roll in powdered sugar.

Addie G. Wood, Coushatta, Louisiana

CONFEDERATE COFFEE CAKE

1 c. sugar	2 tsp. baking powder
Butter	Nutmeg
1/2 c. milk	Cinnamon to taste
3 eggs	1/2 c. chopped nuts
1 1/2 c. flour	

Cream sugar and 1/2 cup butter in a bowl. Add milk and eggs and mix well. Sift the flour, baking powder and dash of nutmeg together and stir into the creamed mixture. Pour into a well-greased loaf pan and sprinkle with small amount of nutmeg, cinnamon, nuts and additional sugar. Dot with butter. Bake at 350 degrees for 20 minutes.

Cheryl Burton, Huntsville, Alabama

PINEAPPLE COFFEE CAKE

3 tbsp. cornstarch	3/4 c. water
1/2 c. sugar	1 beaten egg yolk
1 can crushed pineapple	

Combine the cornstarch and sugar in a saucepan. Add the pineapple and water and mix well. Cook over low heat until thick, stirring frequently. Add egg yolk and cool.

Dough

1 tbsp. sugar	2 1/2 c. sifted flour
1 1/2 pkg. yeast	1 c. butter or margarine
2/3 c. lukewarm milk	3 beaten egg yolks

Dissolve the sugar and yeast in milk in a bowl and set aside. Place the flour in a bowl and cut in the butter. Stir in the yeast mixture and egg yolks. Roll out half the dough into a rectangle and place on a cookie sheet. Spread with pineapple mixture. Roll out remaining dough into a rectangle and place on pineapple mixture. Let rise for 1 hour. Bake at 300 degrees for 30 to 45 minutes or until light brown.

Icing

4 1/2 tbsp. sugar	2/3 c. shortening
2 tbsp. water	1 tsp. vanilla
2 1/2 c. confectioners' sugar	Ground nuts to taste
1 egg	

Mix the sugar and water in a saucepan and cook until thick. Mix confectioners' sugar and egg in a bowl, then pour in hot syrup gradually, beating constantly. Add the shortening and vanilla and beat until firm. Spread on cake and sprinkle with nuts.

Mrs. Sandra Shears, Elizabeth, West Virginia

CREPES SUZETTE NEW ORLEANS

2 eggs	1 c. cake flour
1 1/2 c. milk	1 wine glass white wine or brandy
Grated rind of 1/2 lemon	12 lumps sugar
1/4 tsp. salt	Juice and grated rind of 1 orange
Powdered sugar	1/2 c. melted butter

Beat the eggs in a bowl until lemon colored, then stir in milk, lemon rind and salt. Sift 1 tablespoon powdered sugar with flour into a bowl and beat in milk mixture slowly. Drop by tablespoonfuls on a hot, greased grill. Fry over medium heat until golden brown on both sides. Pour wine into a chafing dish and heat. Mix the sugar and orange juice and add to wine. Add the orange rind and butter and cover. Cook until thick. Dip pancakes in sauce and roll. Sprinkle with powdered sugar and serve immediately. 8 servings.

Mrs. Walter Kuefel, New Orleans, Louisiana

STRAWBERRY CREPES

4 eggs	1 tsp. vanilla
1/2 c. milk	2 tbsp. sugar
1/2 c. water	1 tsp. grated lemon rind (opt.)
Melted butter	Powdered sugar
2 tbsp. cognac	Fresh sweetened strawberries
1 c. flour	Whipped cream
3/4 tsp. salt	

Place the eggs, milk, water, 2 tablespoons butter, cognac, flour, salt, vanilla, sugar and lemon rind in a blender container and blend until smooth. Let stand at room temperature for 30 minutes. Heat a 7-inch skillet and brush with butter. Pour in enough batter to cover bottom of skillet, turning and tilting skillet. Brown on 1 side and keep warm until all crepes are prepared. Sprinkle browned side of crepes with powdered sugar and place 1 spoon strawberries in center of each. Fold envelope fashion and place 1 spoon strawberries on top of each crepe. Cover with whipped cream and garnish with whole strawberries. 6 servings.

Mrs. Sam Nettles, Birmingham, Alabama

SWEET DESSERT CREPES

2 c. milk	1/4 c. sugar
2 c. flour	1 c. melted butter
4 eggs, separated	Confectioners' sugar

Blend the milk and flour in a mixing bowl, then add the egg yolks, one at a time, mixing well after each addition. Add the sugar and mix well. Add the butter and blend thoroughly. Beat egg whites until stiff and fold into the batter. Refrigerate for several hours, then stir well just before cooking. Pour 1 1/2 tablespoons of the batter into a hot, ungreased skillet and tilt in a circular motion until bottom of the skillet is covered. Increase heat for several seconds then reduce heat. Cook for 1 minute. Turn with a wide spatula and cook for 1 minute on the other side.

Remove to a warm platter and dust with confectioners' sugar. Repeat until all batter is used. Crepes may be filled with desired filling or served as accompaniment to dessert. 20 servings.

Ethel Moorman, Phenix City, Alabama

APPEL OLIEKOLDEN

1 pkg. hot roll mix	3 eggs, well beaten
1 c. sugar	1 c. peeled cubed green apples
1/2 tsp. nutmeg	1/2 c. raisins
1/2 c. orange juice	

Combine flour from roll mix with sugar and nutmeg in a bowl and mix well. Heat orange juice to lukewarm and add yeast from roll mix. Stir until dissolved and add eggs, apples and raisins. Mix well. Add flour mixture and blend well. Knead on a lightly floured board until smooth. Cover and let rise until doubled in bulk. Punch down and knead lightly. Roll out 1/2 inch thick and cut with 3-inch doughnut cutter. Let rise for 30 minutes. Fry in deep fat at 375 degrees for 2 to 3 minutes on each side. Drain well and roll in colored sugar, if desired.

Mrs. H. J. Kolinek, Kenedy, Texas

RAISED DOUGHNUTS

1 c. scalded milk	2 tbsp. lukewarm water
2/3 c. sugar	5 c. (about) flour
3 tbsp. shortening	2 eggs, well beaten
1 tsp. salt	1 tsp. nutmeg
1 pkg. dry yeast	Powdered sugar

Mix the milk, sugar, shortening and salt in a mixing bowl and cool to lukewarm. Dissolve yeast in water and stir into milk mixture. Add 2 cups flour and mix well. Set in warm place to rise until light. Add the eggs, nutmeg and enough remaining flour to make a soft dough. Cover and let rise until doubled in bulk. Knead until elastic. Roll out 1/2 inch thick on lightly floured board and cut with doughnut cutter. Cover and set in warm place to rise until doubled in bulk. Fry in deep, hot fat until puffy and brown. Turn and brown on other side. Drain on absorbent paper and sprinkle with powdered sugar while warm. 30 servings.

Mrs. Elsie S. Trader, Angier, North Carolina

FRUIT DROP DOUGHNUTS

2 eggs	2 tsp. baking powder
1/2 c. sugar	1/2 tsp. salt
2 tbsp. salad oil	1/2 c. orange juice
2 c. flour	2 tsp. grated orange rind

Beat the eggs in a bowl until thick and lemon colored, then add sugar and oil gradually, beating constantly. Sift the flour, baking powder and salt together and add to egg mixture alternately with mixture of orange juice and grated rind. Drop by heaping teaspoonfuls into hot, deep fat and fry until brown, turning once. Drain. 2 dozen.

Evelyn M. Garrett, Memphis, Tennessee

CINNAMON-TOPPED OATMEAL MUFFINS

1 c. sifted all-purpose flour	1/2 c. raisins
1/4 c. sugar	3 tbsp. melted shortening
3 tsp. baking powder	1 egg, beaten
1/2 tsp. salt	1 c. milk
1 c. oatmeal	

Preheat oven to 425 degrees. Sift the flour, sugar, baking powder and salt together into a bowl and stir in oatmeal and raisins. Add the shortening, egg and milk and stir just until dry ingredients are moistened. Fill greased muffin cups 2/3 full.

Topping

2 tbsp. sugar	1 tsp. cinnamon
2 tsp. all-purpose flour	1 tsp. melted butter

Combine all ingredients and sprinkle on batter. Bake for about 15 minutes. 12 muffins.

Carolyn Zenker, Lawrenceburg, Tennessee

RAISIN-OATMEAL MUFFINS

3/4 c. sifted flour	1 c. dark seedless raisins
2 tsp. baking powder	2 eggs, slightly beaten
3/4 tsp. salt	1/2 c. milk
1/3 c. sugar	1/4 c. cooking oil
1 c. rolled oats	

Sift the flour with baking powder, salt and sugar into a bowl and stir in the oats and raisins. Combine the eggs, milk and oil and add to flour mixture. Mix lightly with fork just until dry ingredients are moistened and fill greased muffin cups 2/3 full. Bake at 400 degrees for about 20 minutes. 12 muffins.

CRANBERRY MUFFINS

1 c. chopped fresh cranberries	1/4 tsp. salt
3/4 c. sugar	1 egg, beaten
2 c. sifted flour	3/4 c. buttermilk
3/4 tsp. soda	1/4 c. melted shortening

Combine the cranberries and 1/2 cup sugar. Sift flour, soda, salt and remaining sugar together into a mixing bowl and make a well in the center. Mix the egg, buttermilk and shortening and add to dry ingredients all at once. Stir until mixed. Add the cranberry mixture and mix lightly. Fill greased muffin cups 2/3 full. Bake in 400-degree oven for 20 minutes.

Mrs. Jessie Sue Smith, Cullman, Alabama

NUT BREAD

1 c. sugar	3 tsp. baking powder
2 eggs, separated	1 c. milk
2 c. flour	1 c. chopped pecans or walnuts

Combine the sugar and egg yolks in a bowl and beat well. Sift flour and baking powder together and add to the sugar mixture alternately with milk. Fold in beaten egg whites, then fold in the pecans. Pour into greased loaf pan. Bake at 300 degrees for 1 hour.

Mrs. George S. Westlake, Pensacola, Florida

HONEY-NUT BREAD

2 c. flour	1 egg, beaten
3 tsp. baking powder	1/2 c. honey
1/2 tsp. salt	1/2 c. milk
1/2 c. coarsely chopped nuts	2 tbsp. melted butter

Sift the dry ingredients together into a bowl and stir in nuts. Combine the egg, honey, milk and butter. Add to the flour mixture and stir until dry ingredients are just moistened. Pour into a greased loaf pan. Bake at 350 degrees for 45 to 50 minutes.

Teresa Davison, Finley, Tennessee

MINCEMEAT ROLL

1 1/2 c. flour	1/2 c. crushed pineapple
2 tsp. baking powder	2 c. mincemeat
3 tbsp. (rounded) shortening	2 c. (packed) light brown sugar
Milk	2 c. water

Mix the flour and baking powder in a bowl and cut in the shortening. Stir in enough milk for stiff dough. Roll out 1/3 inch thick in oblong shape. Mix pineapple with mincemeat and spread on dough. Roll as for jelly roll and place in a baking pan. Mix the brown sugar and water in a saucepan and bring to a boil. Pour over the roll. Bake in 350-degree oven for 45 minutes and garnish with maraschino cherries. 8 servings.

Mrs. James H. Lambert, Butler, Kentucky

GLAZED CHERRY-APRICOT COFFEE RING

2 pkg. dry yeast
1/2 c. warm water
3/4 c. scalded milk
1 c. softened butter or margarine
1/4 c. sugar
2 eggs, slightly beaten
1 tsp. grated lemon peel

4 1/2 c. sifted all-purpose flour
2 tbsp. melted butter or margarine
Cherry-Apricot Filling
1/3 c. apricot preserves, melted
1 tbsp. cold milk
1/2 c. confectioners' sugar

Dissolve the yeast in water. Cool the scalded milk to lukewarm. Add the yeast, softened butter, sugar, eggs, lemon peel and flour and mix until blended. Cover tightly and refrigerate overnight. Divide dough in half. Roll out each half on a floured surface to a 12 x 8-inch rectangle and brush with melted butter. Spread half the Cherry-Apricot Filling over each rectangle and roll from long side as for jelly roll. Seal edges. Place in ring on greased baking sheet and seal ends together. Cut 2/3 way into rings with scissors at 2-inch intervals, turning each section on its side. Cover with towel and let rise in warm place, free from draft, for 1 hour or until doubled in bulk. Bake in 350-degree oven for 20 to 25 minutes. Brush with apricot preserves. Mix cold milk and confectioners' sugar and drizzle over coffee rings.

Cherry-Apricot Filling

1 c. dried apricots
2 c. water
1/2 c. sugar

1/2 c. chopped nuts
1 8-oz. jar red maraschino
    cherries

Place the apricots in a bowl and pour the water over apricots. Let set until apricots are soft. Drain the apricots, chop and add the sugar and nuts. Drain the cherries and cut in halves. Add to apricot mixture and mix well.

INDEX

PHOTOGRAPHY CREDITS: Florida Citrus Commission; Knox Gelatine, Incorporated; The Nestle Company; Jell-O Whip 'n Chill; Baker's German's Sweet Chocolate; Baker's Angel Flake Coconut; California Strawberry Advisory Board; National Cherry Growers and Industries Foundation; American Dairy Council; The American Spice Trade Association; Processed Apples Institute; National Biscuit Company; Pet Milk, Incorporated; Standard Brands: Fleischmann's Yeast, Fleischmann's Margarine, Royal Puddings and Gelatines; Quaker Oats; Standard FRuit and Steamship Company: Cabana Bananas; Best Foods: A Division of Corn Products, International; National Dairy Council; Filbert/Hazelnut Institute; McCormick and Company; Armour and Company; Sunkist Growers; United Fresh Fruit and Vegetable Association; Grandma's West Indies Molasses Sugar Information Institute; American Dry Milk Institute; The Bordon Company Cling Peach Advisory Board; Jell-O Pudding and Pie Filling; Diamond Walnut Kitchens; Evaporated Milk Association; Ocean Spray Cranberries, Incorporated; Keith Thomas Company; California Avocado Advisory Board; Angostura-Wuppermann Corporation; National Peanut Council; California Raisins Advisory Board.

Printed in the United States of America.